FULL GUIDE TO HABITS

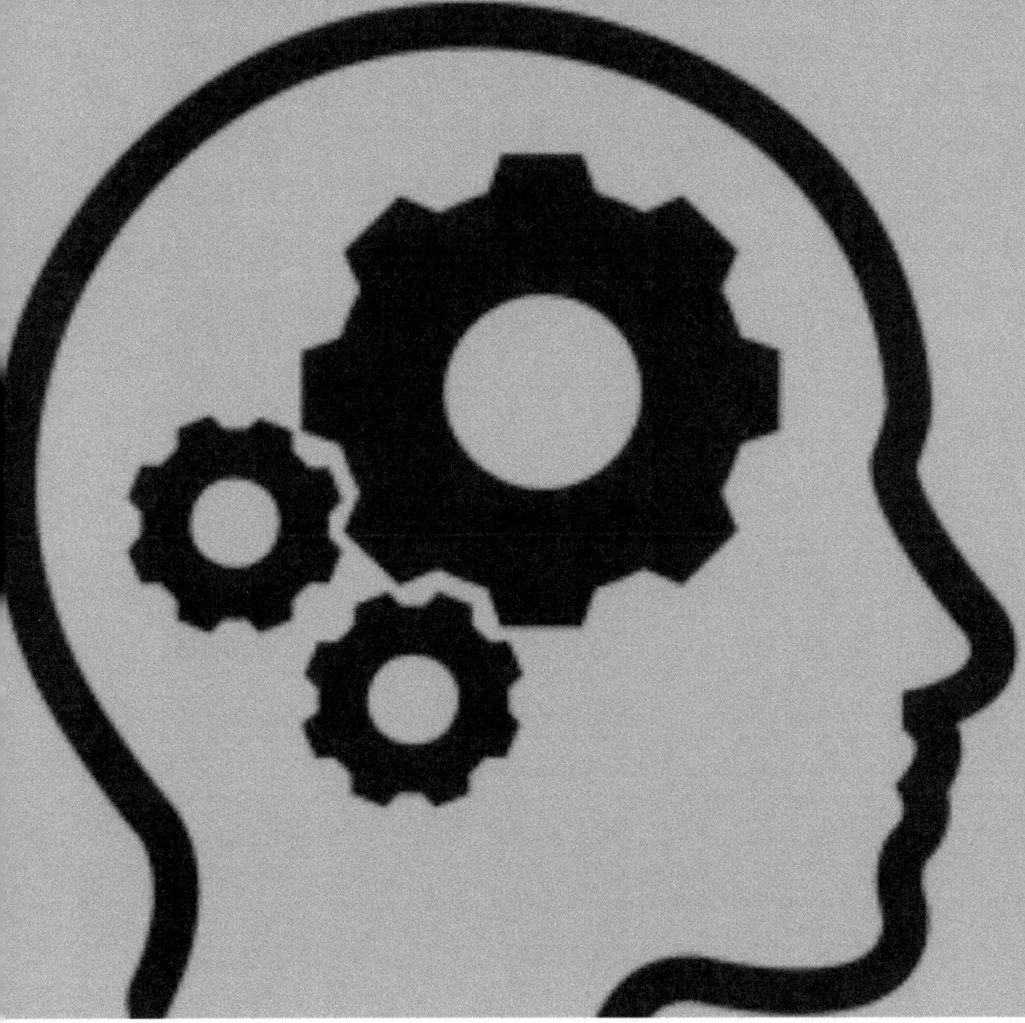

Table of Content

Introduction - Page 2

Chapter 1: The Science of Habits - Page 4

Chapter 2: The Habit Loop - Page 13

Chapter 3: Identifying Your Habits - Page 24

Chapter 4: Building New Habits - Page 35

Chapter 5: Breaking Bad Habits - Page 47

Chapter 6: The Power of Environment - Page 56

Chapter 7: Habit Stacking and Automation - Page 65

Chapter 8: Case Studies of Transformation - Page 73

Chapter 9: Maintaining and Evolving Habits - Page 85

Appendix - Page 98

Introduction

Habits are the invisible architecture of our everyday lives. They shape our behaviors, guide our choices, and ultimately influence our destinies. Whether we realize it or not, our days are filled with small, seemingly inconsequential decisions that, when aggregated, define the course of our lives. From the moment we wake up to the moment we fall asleep, we engage in many routines—some beneficial, others detrimental. Understanding the power of these habits is crucial not only for personal growth but also for achieving our long-term goals.

At their core, habits are neurological patterns established through repetition. When we act consistently over time, our brains form pathways that facilitate easier recall and execution of that behavior. This phenomenon explains why habits can be difficult to change; once a behavior becomes ingrained in our neural circuitry, it often operates below our conscious awareness. However, by investigating the science behind habits and understanding how they function, we empower ourselves to take control of our lives, instilling positive habits while dismantling those that hinder our progress.

The concept of the "habit loop"—a framework introduced by researcher Charles Duhigg in his groundbreaking book, "The Power of Habit"—is fundamental to understanding the dynamics of habits. The habit loop consists of three key components: cue, routine, and reward. The cue serves as a trigger that signals the brain to initiate a specific behavior, which is the routine. Following this routine, there is typically a reward that reinforces the behavior, creating a cycle that encourages repetition. By analyzing these components, we can better understand the factors that contribute to habit formation and make informed decisions about modifying our routines for the better.

In this exploration of habits, we will delve into the science behind habit formation, examining the neurological underpinnings that drive our behaviors. Understanding the brain's role can help demystify why habits exist and why they can be so hard to change. The basal ganglia, a cluster of nuclei located deep within the brain, plays a crucial role in the development of habits, while the prefrontal cortex is responsible for decision-making and self-control. A delicate balance between these regions determines the extent to which habits govern our actions.

As we embark on this journey of understanding, a critical aspect will be self-awareness. Identifying and evaluating our habits is the first step toward positive change. This book will provide tools and techniques to help you track your habits, recognize patterns, and assess their impact on your life. The process of self-reflection can reveal insights that are essential for cultivating new, healthier habits while eliminating those that no longer serve you.

The creation of new habits requires deliberate intention and dedication. Small, incremental changes can lead to significant transformations over time. By incorporating strategies such as the "two-minute rule," which advocates for starting with just two minutes of new behavior, we can lower the psychological barrier to initiating change. Consistency is key; the more frequently we engage in a new routine, the more likely it is to become a lasting habit.

Conversely, breaking bad habits necessitates a proactive approach. Recognizing the cues and rewards associated with negative behaviors is essential for disrupting the cycle. This book will offer valuable insights into techniques for identifying bad habits and practical strategies for replacing them with more positive alternatives. The support of a robust social network can provide the necessary encouragement and accountability during this challenging process.

The environment we inhabit plays a significant role in habit formation as well. Our physical surroundings and social circles can either facilitate or hinder our progress. By consciously reshaping our environments and surrounding ourselves with positive influences, we can create a fertile ground for successful habit formation. Simple adjustments, such as decluttering our spaces or altering our routines to minimize exposure to triggers, can lead to profound changes in our behavior.

Throughout this book, you will encounter compelling case studies of individuals who have redefined their lives through an understanding of habits. These narratives illustrate the potential for transformation that lies within the habit loop. They serve as powerful reminders that change is possible and that with commitment, anyone can cultivate the habits necessary for achieving their personal and professional goals.

In addition to discussing how to build and break habits, we will also explore the journey of maintaining and evolving them over time. Habits should not remain static; rather, they should adapt and grow as we progress through different stages of life. Embracing a growth mindset regarding our habits empowers us to continuously reflect on our practices and adjust as necessary.

As we embark on this exploration of the power of habit, this book will serve as a comprehensive guide for transforming your relationship with habits. By the end, you will possess the tools and insights needed to design a life that aligns with your aspirations and values. The journey toward self-improvement is multifaceted and may require patience and perseverance, but rest assured, the rewards of mastering your habits are immeasurable.

Chapter 1: The Science of Habits

Habits are fundamental building blocks of human behavior, intricately woven into the fabric of our daily lives. To comprehend the power of habits, one must first understand how they are formed and the neurological processes that underpin them. The formation of a habit is not an arbitrary event; it involves complex physiological and psychological mechanisms that dictate how we act in consistent and automatic ways.

The Habit Formation Process

At its core, habit formation can be likened to the development of well-trodden paths in a forest. Initially, the path may be faint and require effort to traverse; however, with repeated passage, it becomes more defined and easier to navigate. Similarly, when we first engage in a behavior, our brains must exert considerable cognitive effort. Over time, as the behavior is repeated, the necessary neural pathways are strengthened, leading to automaticity— the ability to execute the behavior with little conscious thought.

The behaviorist perspective, grounded in principles established by psychologists such as B.F. Skinner, suggests that habits are formed through reinforcement. When a behavior is followed by a positive outcome or reward, the likelihood of that behavior being repeated increases. In the context of habit formation, this cycle can be framed using the three components of the habit loop: cue, routine, and reward. This framework was notably articulated by Charles Duhigg and has become a foundational concept in the study of habits.

Neurological Processes: The Habit Loop

1. **Cue**: The first element of the habit loop is the cue. A cue, or trigger, is a stimulus that initiates the habit. It can be an internal or external signal, such as a specific time of day, an emotional state, or even environmental stimuli. Research has shown that cues activate specific neural circuits, prompting the brain to initiate a routine that it associates with the cue.

2. **Routine**: The routine is the behavior executed in response to the cue. At this stage, the activity becomes progressively automatic as it is repeated. When a habit is first formed, the prefrontal cortex—the brain's region responsible for decision-making and complex cognitive behavior—is heavily engaged. However, as the habit is reinforced and repeated, control shifts to the basal ganglia, a cluster of nuclei linked to the regulation of voluntary motor control and procedural

learning. The basal ganglia enable the brain to conserve energy by automating behaviors, allowing individuals to engage in complex tasks without heavy cognitive load.

3. **Reward**: Finally, the reward is the positive reinforcement that follows the routine. The brain releases neurotransmitters, such as dopamine, in response to the reward, creating a sense of pleasure and satisfaction associated with the behavior. This chemical reinforcement not only solidifies the neural pathway associated with the habit but also engrains the cue-routine-reward sequence in the brain, making it more likely for the habit to be repeated in the future.

The Role of Neuroplasticity

Central to our understanding of habit formation is the concept of neuroplasticity—the brain's remarkable ability to reorganize itself by forming new neural connections throughout life. Neuroplasticity allows our brains to adapt to new experiences, learn new information, and change our behaviors. When a habit is formed, the repeated activation of specific neural pathways results in structural changes in the brain. This plasticity is what enables us to establish new habits and modify existing ones.

However, neuroplasticity also accounts for the challenge of changing unwanted habits. As certain pathways are reinforced through repetition, they become deeply ingrained and resistant to alteration. This phenomenon explains why breaking a bad habit can be so difficult; the neural architecture supporting that habit must be reshaped, requiring conscious effort and often repeated attempts.

The Impact of Environment

While the intrinsic neurological processes underpinning habit formation are critical, environmental factors also play a significant role. The context in which a habit is formed influences the strength and persistence of the habit. For example, if an individual associates a particular environment, such as a specific café, with the routine of drinking coffee, the environmental cue becomes intertwined with the habit. Consequently, merely entering the café can trigger cravings for coffee, demonstrating how context can evoke habitual behaviors.

Understanding environmental cues extends beyond physical spaces. Social and cultural influences can also affect habit formation. The behaviors of peers, family, and societal norms can serve as significant motivators or deterrents in the establishment of habits. This interplay between neurological processes and environmental factors emphasizes the multifaceted nature of habit formation and change.

Conclusion: The Intersection of Science and Action

The science of habits provides invaluable insights into why we behave the way we do and how we can harness the power of habit to our advantage. By understanding the nuanced interplay of cues, routines, and rewards, we can begin to identify the habits that shape our lives and apply scientific principles to effect positive change.

In subsequent chapters, we will explore strategies for cultivating new habits, breaking free from detrimental ones, and creating an environment conducive to positive behavioral change. With a solid understanding of the science underlying habits, we will equip ourselves with the knowledge to take actionable steps toward transforming our behaviors and, ultimately, our lives. Understanding the chemistry and mechanics of habit formation is the first step in reclaiming control over our actions and establishing a future in line with our aspirations.

When exploring the formation of habits, it is imperative to recognize the crucial roles played by specific regions of the brain, particularly the basal ganglia and the prefrontal cortex. Understanding these areas not only reveals how habits are entrenched within our neural architecture but also illustrates the intricate balance between instinctive behavior and conscious decision-making.

The basal ganglia, a group of nuclei located deep within the cerebral hemispheres, serve as a fundamental hub in the brain's reward circuit. These structures are vital for the formation and retrieval of habits, as they facilitate the automatic execution of learned behaviors once they have been ingrained through repetition. The primary role of the basal ganglia in habit formation can be summed up as the consolidation of actions into routines that eventually require little to no conscious thought.

When a behavior is repeated frequently enough, the basal ganglia effectively take over the management of that behavior. This means that, over time, the intricate steps involved in acting—whether it's brushing your teeth, exercising, or even more complex tasks like driving—transition from being externally driven and conscious efforts to automatic actions that can be performed with minimal cognitive involvement. This shift occurs because the neural pathways associated with these habits become strengthened and refined, allowing our brains to execute them almost effortlessly.

The transformation happens through a process called synaptic plasticity, wherein the connections between neurons change in response to activity. As specific neurons fire together repeatedly—when engaging in a habit—the strength of synaptic connections between these neurons increases. This biological underpinning is why habits can become so deeply embedded; the more frequently the basal ganglia are activated by a particular routine, the less active involvement from the prefrontal cortex is required.

In contrast, the prefrontal cortex, located at the front part of the brain, is responsible for higher-level cognitive functions, including decision-making, impulse control, and critical thinking. This area is essential for assessing situations and determining appropriate responses—functions that are vital for goal setting and self-regulation. While the basal ganglia handles the mechanics of habitual behavior, the prefrontal cortex is engaged in the executive functions that help us deliberate and reflect on our actions.

At the intersection of these two regions lies a delicate balancing act: the prefrontal cortex manages our conscious intentions and ability to adapt our behaviors based on circumstances. At the same time, the basal ganglia facilitate the smooth running of routines established as habits. When a decision needs to be made, such as whether to stick to a healthy diet or to indulge in a treat, the prefrontal cortex performs a risk-benefit analysis based on long-term goals, weighing it against the immediate reward that the basal ganglia may automatically signal.

This dynamic can elucidate why breaking a bad habit can often feel like an uphill battle. The more entrenched a habit becomes, the more the basal ganglia push for automatic responses that are difficult to resist. Breaking free from these ingrained routines often requires a significant amount of cognitive effort from the prefrontal cortex, necessitating a conscious redirection of behavior. This struggle is compounded when environmental cues trigger the habitual response, drawing us back into the automatic pathways established in the basal ganglia.

Research has shed light on the functional interplay between these two brain regions. For example, studies using neuroimaging techniques, such as fMRI, have shown that when individuals engage in habitual tasks, there tends to be increased activity in the basal ganglia, while the prefrontal cortex exhibits reduced activation. This shift suggests that as behaviors become habitual, they increasingly rely on the basal ganglia, resulting in less involvement from the conscious, reflective aspects of the brain.

Moreover, this understanding has implications for interventions aimed at habit change. The idea that the basal ganglia support automaticity means that simply wishing to change a behavior is often insufficient; a more proactive approach is required. This can involve implementing strategies that align the prefrontal cortex's goal-setting abilities with methods that disrupt or alter the habitual pathways carved in the basal ganglia. Cognitive-behavioral techniques, mindfulness practices, and environmental modifications can be utilized to create new patterns of behavior that are not only appealing but also engaging enough to invoke the necessary prefrontal cortex activation to challenge entrenched habits.

In conclusion, the relationship between the basal ganglia and the prefrontal cortex is foundational to our understanding of habits. These areas of the brain exemplify the dual nature of habit formation: an instinctive, automatic component supported by the basal ganglia and a conscious, goal-oriented aspect governed by the prefrontal cortex. By appreciating how these regions interact, we can better navigate the complexities of our routines, striving toward habits that promote our well-being while navigating the often turbulent waters of change. This knowledge lays the groundwork for meaningful strategies to foster positive habits, break free from detrimental ones, and cultivate a profound sense of self-awareness in our journey toward personal growth.

As we delve deeper into the science of habits, it is essential to examine various studies that illuminate the brain's responses to habits and the intricate workings of our neurological systems. These studies not only bolster our understanding of how habits form and become entrenched but also reveal the profound impact they have on our daily lives and decision-making processes.

One of the seminal studies in this area was conducted by researchers at MIT, led by John P. Rice and colleagues, who investigated the neural mechanisms involved in the formation of habits. Their work focused on the role of the basal ganglia in habit formation through a series of experiments involving rats. The researchers trained the rats to navigate a maze to receive a food reward. Once the rats had learned the task, they switched the environment to introduce new variables, such as changing the placement of the reward or altering the path. Observing the rats' brain activity during these trials, the researchers found that the bilateral striatum—part of the basal ganglia—was highly active as the rats displayed habitual behavior in the maze. This study highlighted the brain's adaptability and the strong association between the basal ganglia and automaticity in behavior.

In another groundbreaking experiment, a team at Duke University, led by neuroscientist Michael M. Frank, examined the effects of habit formation on decision-making. Using functional MRI scans, the researchers observed participants as they engaged in a task requiring them to make choices that led to rewards, such as monetary gains. The results indicated that as participants repeated the task over multiple trials, there was a notable shift in brain activity. Initially, the prefrontal cortex was active as participants evaluated their options and calculated potential outcomes. However, as they became more familiar with the task, activities shifted predominantly to the basal ganglia, indicating that decisions had transitioned into a habitual response. This finding underscored how the brain becomes more efficient by relying on habits, freeing up cognitive resources for other tasks.

Additionally, a study published in the journal *Nature* explored the role of reinforcement and reward in habit formation. Researchers found that when subjects were conditioned through a reward system—receiving positive feedback for certain behaviors—the brain exhibited heightened activity in the nucleus accumbens, a component of the basal ganglia associated with the reward circuit. This activation reinforced the behavior, forming a powerful connection between the cue (the condition leading to the behavior), the routine (the behavior itself), and the reward (the positive feedback). The findings demonstrated how habits are not only formed through repetition but also deeply rooted in our brain's response to rewards, which highlights the potential for leveraging positive reinforcement to foster desirable habits.

Moreover, studies on addiction provide further insight into the brain's response to habits. Research led by neuroscientists at the University of Cambridge examined the similarities between the mechanisms of habitual behavior and the compulsive behaviors seen in addiction. By utilizing neuroimaging to track brain activity in individuals with substance use disorders, the study revealed that both habit formation and addiction engage overlapping neural circuits, particularly those involving the basal ganglia. The distorted reward pathways in individuals with addictions illustrated how habitual behaviors could become maladaptive, resulting in compulsive actions despite negative consequences. This research opened avenues for understanding how addiction can be reframed as a failure of habit control, emphasizing the critical need for interventions that target the underlying neural mechanisms.

Interestingly, a parallel line of research investigates the effect of stress and its impact on habits. Studies have shown that elevated stress levels can alter the reactivity of the prefrontal cortex, reducing its capacity for self-regulation and decision-making. When under stress, individuals are more likely to revert to established habitual responses, often prioritizing immediate rewards over long-term benefits. For instance, a study published in *Psychological Science* demonstrated that participants who experienced acute stress were more prone to indulge in unhealthy eating habits, such as consuming high-calorie snacks. These results indicate that the interaction between stress and the brain's response to habitual behavior can significantly derail intentions and promote undesirable habits.

Furthermore, another notable study conducted at the University of Southern California, involving a longitudinal analysis of participants' brain activity and self-reported habits, revealed compelling evidence linking habitual behavior to neuroplasticity—the brain's ability to reorganize itself by forming new neural connections throughout life. As participants engaged in specific beneficial habits, such as consistent exercise and mindfulness practices, researchers noted structural changes in the brain, particularly in areas associated with impulse control and emotional regulation. This provided promising insights into how individuals can cultivate a healthier lifestyle through intentional habit formation and highlighted the brain's remarkable ability to adapt over time.

Lastly, the well-known concept of "cue-induced cravings" has received considerable attention in recent years. Research has shown that exposure to certain cues—environmental or contextual stimuli associated with previous rewarding experiences—can trigger cravings for habits, even when the context has changed. A study examining food cues demonstrated that merely seeing images of high-calorie foods activated the brain's reward centers in the basal ganglia, leading to increased cravings for those foods. These findings have significant implications for habit-breaking strategies, revealing the necessity of addressing environmental triggers in the quest to dismantle detrimental habits.

In conclusion, studies regarding the brain's response to habits illustrate the remarkable interplay between neurological processes, habitual behavior, and environmental influences. The research collectively emphasizes the powerful role of the basal ganglia in automating behaviors and the prefrontal cortex's essential function in decision-making and self-regulation. As we uncover the neural mechanisms underpinning our habitual actions, we not only gain insight into the challenges of habit formation and change but also identify potential pathways for developing effective strategies for cultivating positive habits and breaking free from those that hinder our growth. Understanding these processes empowers individuals to harness the science of habits to shape their futures, making informed choices that align with their goals and aspirations.

Chapter 2: The Habit Loop

To fully understand the dynamics of habit formation, we must first dissect the fundamental components that make up what is known as the habit loop: cue, routine, and reward. First, we will focus on the first of these elements—cue, which serves as the trigger that initiates our behavioral patterns. By identifying and analyzing cues, we can gain valuable insights into the driving forces behind our habits.

Cues are the signals that prompt us to act, whether they are external stimuli from our environment or internal signals related to our thoughts and feelings. These triggers can be as straightforward as the sound of an alarm clock in the morning, the sight of a running shoe by the door, or even a nagging feeling of stress that compels us to seek comfort through food. Understanding the nature of these cues is crucial because they set the stage for the routines that follow.

Cues can be categorized into five distinct types: location, time, emotional state, other people, and specific actions. Each of these categories offers a unique perspective on how our environment and state of mind influence our behaviors:

1. **Location**: Where we are physically situated can heavily influence our habits. The office might trigger a work-focused routine, while home may lead to relaxation or entertainment habits. By examining the places we frequent, we can pinpoint which environments foster positive or negative behaviors.

2. **Time**: The time of day plays a significant role in our habits. For instance, many people find that they perform certain tasks more effectively in the morning versus the evening. Journaling, exercising, or even indulging in unhealthy snacks can become routine based on the time of day alone. Recognizing these patterns can help us align our activities with our natural rhythms.

3. **Emotional State**: Our emotional well-being directly impacts our choices. Feelings of happiness, boredom, anxiety, or sadness can act as powerful cues that lead us toward specific actions. For example, someone feeling stressed may gravitate toward unhealthy eating as a coping mechanism. Understanding this link allows us to address the roots of our habits rather than just the surface behaviors.

4. **Other People**: The influence of social interactions cannot be underestimated. The presence of certain friends or colleagues can evoke desired or undesired habits. Social cues often trigger behaviors, whether it's joining in on a workout session or indulging in unhealthy snacking during a gathering. Recognizing the impacts of our social circles can help us navigate our behaviors more effectively.

5. **Specific Actions**: Sometimes, a preceding behavior can serve as a cue for the next action. For instance, brushing our teeth can trigger the habit of flossing. Being aware of these sequential cues enables us to create a chain of positive habits, enhancing the overall effectiveness of our routines.

As we delve deeper into the realm of cues, self-reflection becomes our most powerful tool. Keeping a habit journal may help in identifying specific triggers and understanding their impact. This practice encourages greater awareness and enables us to take proactive steps toward making intentional changes.

Once a cue has been identified, the next integral component of the habit loop is the routine itself— the behavior or set of actions that follow the trigger. This phase of the loop encompasses the actual execution of the habit, a process that can be complex and multilayered. Understanding the nature of routines is crucial, as they represent the tangible outcomes of our habitual patterns and can significantly influence our daily lives.

At its core, a routine is a series of actions that we repeat in response to a specific cue. These actions can range from simple, almost automatic behaviors to more intricate sequences that require planning and engagement. For example, the routine that follows waking up might be as simple as brushing your teeth and brewing a cup of coffee, or it could involve a structured morning workout and meditation session. The diversity in routines illustrates the unique ways individuals respond to their cues, shaped by personal values, goals, and lifestyles.

Analyzing our routines offers substantial insights into how we navigate our days and the effectiveness of our habits. One of the first steps in this analysis is to observe which routines yield positive outcomes and which ones may lead to undesirable consequences. This process requires an honest reflection on our behaviors and their impact on our physical, emotional, and social well-being.

Breaking down the routines into specific actions allows us to discern patterns that may not be immediately visible. Ask yourself: What exactly do I do when I encounter a particular cue? Is there a sequence of actions that I follow, or do I chaotically react? Recognizing these patterns is essential for understanding not only how a routine forms but also how it can be modified or replaced.

Moreover, routines can vary in complexity. Some may comprise a single action, like grabbing a chocolate bar when feeling stressed, while others can be multi-faceted, involving a combination of behaviors. For instance, consider the routine of preparing for a big presentation: it may involve setting aside time to research the topic, crafting a compelling narrative, practicing delivery, and even visualizing success. In this more elaborate routine, each action reinforces the overall goal of mastering the presentation.

Identifying the emotional and psychological state during the routine can further enrich our analysis. Often, the actions we take are governed by deeper desires or fears. For example, engaging in retail therapy may provide temporary relief from stress, leading to behaviors that serve to soothe immediate discomfort but may compound financial stress in the long run. Recognizing these emotional ties can open avenues for reframing our routines.

Another critical aspect to consider is how environmental context influences routines. The environment acts as a silent yet powerful conspirator in the habit loop. A workplace filled with unhealthy snacks might trigger a routine of excessive snacking, while a dedicated workout space can encourage a consistent exercise routine. By analyzing and, if necessary, restructuring our environments, we can create contexts that foster beneficial routines while buffering against detrimental ones.

The consistency of the routine also plays a significant role in habit formation. Psychological studies suggest that the more frequently a specific behavior is enacted in response to a cue, the stronger the connection becomes between the cue and the routine. This creates an almost automatic response; the brain begins to associate the cue with the established routine, making it increasingly hard to disrupt. For example, consider how an individual who consistently smokes a cigarette with their morning coffee may find it challenging to break the habit since both actions are now intertwined neurologically.

To disrupt a negative routine, one must identify alternative behaviors that offer similar rewards but are aligned with healthier outcomes. This can often feel daunting, as it requires not only a change in action but also in thinking. For instance, if snacking out of boredom is the routine, replacing it with a more constructive behavior—such as taking a short walk or practicing a hobby—can serve to fulfill the underlying desire for a break or distraction in a healthier manner.

An essential part of successfully modifying a routine is the role of rewards, which offer the next step in understanding the habit loop. Often, behaviors are reinforced through the positive feelings or results they produce, creating a desire to repeat them in the future. This interdependence between the routine and its associated reward illustrates why simply recognizing a cue is not enough; without carefully evaluating the routine that follows, we may miss the opportunity for meaningful change.

As we explore the nature of our routines and the behaviors that shape our lives, it becomes imperative to adopt a growth mindset. Embracing the idea that routines can change and evolve opens the door to ongoing personal development. By committing to analyzing and refining our routines regularly, we can shift our focus toward actions that reflect our aspirations rather than those that merely perpetuate old habits.

The reward is a fundamental aspect of the habit loop, which encompasses the core components of cue, routine, and reward. It serves as the driving force that solidifies behaviors and encourages their continuation over time. Delving deeper into the nature of rewards reveals their complexity and significance in our daily lives and their profound impact on habit formation.

At the heart of any habit lies the motivation to repeat a behavior, and this motivation is largely fueled by the anticipation of a reward. The reward can take numerous forms, whether it be physical, psychological, or social. Understanding what constitutes a reward is essential because different individuals are motivated by different things. For one person, a reward may represent the enjoyment of indulging in a favorite dessert after completing a workout, while for another, it might be the satisfaction of checking off a completed task on a to-do list. These variations in perception mean that the reward must resonate with the individual in order to effectively reinforce the habit.

The effectiveness of a reward is often tied to its immediacy. Immediate rewards tend to yield stronger behavioral reinforcement than delayed rewards because they create a more direct connection between the behavior and the positive outcome. When we receive instant gratification after completing a task, the brain quickly associates the action with a pleasurable consequence, which encourages us to repeat that behavior in the future. For example, if someone practices a musical instrument and hears an improvement in their skill right away, the immediate feedback acts as a potent reward, reinforcing their commitment to practice further.

Another critical factor is the nature of the reward itself. Rewards can be classified as extrinsic or intrinsic. Extrinsic rewards are external to the individual and often take the form of tangible incentives, such as money, gifts, or social recognition. These rewards can be particularly motivating, especially in the early stages of habit formation when an individual may struggle to maintain behavior based solely on internal satisfaction. On the other hand, intrinsic rewards stem from internal satisfaction and a sense of accomplishment. These could include feelings of joy after completing a challenging workout or the deep satisfaction one feels from mastering a new skill. Intrinsic rewards tend to foster longer-lasting habit formation since they create an emotional connection to the behavior, making it feel valuable in its own right.

The interplay between intrinsic and extrinsic rewards is important to consider when forming or modifying habits. For instance, when individuals rely heavily on external validation or material incentives, they may experience a decline in motivation once those rewards are removed or no longer effective. In contrast, when the intrinsic elements, such as contentment or pride, are emphasized, individuals are more likely to continue engaging in the behavior even in the absence of explicit rewards. This shift towards intrinsic motivation promotes internalization of the habit and aligns the behavior with personal values and goals.

Moreover, the psychological aspect of rewards cannot be overlooked. Our brains release neurotransmitters, such as dopamine, when we receive a reward, creating feelings of pleasure and satisfaction. This biochemical response reinforces the neural pathways associated with the habit, making it easier to engage in the behavior again in the future. Over time, as we repeat the action and experience the associated reward, those neural pathways become stronger, further embedding the habit in our routine. The sensation of reward becomes not just an external factor but also an internal drive propelling us toward the behavior.

Creating a system of rewards can be instrumental in habit formation, especially when those rewards are meaningful and relevant to the behavior at hand. For example, if someone is trying to build a reading habit, setting up a reward system that involves treating themselves to a nice coffee or enjoying a cozy evening after finishing a certain number of pages can effectively create a positive feedback loop. The act of reading becomes associated with a pleasant experience, reinforcing the desire to continue reading.

It's important to consider the impact of variability in rewards as well. Introducing unpredictability into the reward system can enhance engagement. For instance, when rewards are alternating in nature—some days it might be an intrinsic reward of satisfaction, while other days could involve an extrinsic element like a small prize—it heightens excitement and motivation. This unpredictability can also create a sense of anticipation, making the repetition of the habit more enjoyable and less monotonous.

Lastly, understanding what drives the desire for certain rewards leads to greater clarity in habit modification. When attempting to replace a habit, one must identify what reward the undesirable behavior satisfies and find alternative routines that provide similar, or even better, rewards. For example, if someone struggles with stress eating as a way to feel comforted, exploring healthier strategies to achieve comfort—such as going for a walk, practicing mindfulness, or engaging in a hobby—provides pathways to gain the same emotional fulfillment without the negative consequences associated with the original habit.

Recognizing the pivotal role of the reward within the habit loop allows for a more nuanced approach to building and sustaining positive behaviors. By understanding the psychological, emotional, and practical implications of rewards, individuals can cultivate habits that enrich their lives while fostering a deeper connection to their behaviors and aspirations. This knowledge not only aids in the reinforcement of existing habits but also serves as a guiding principle in the pursuit of personal growth and development.

Habit loops can manifest in various areas of our lives, from personal health to professional productivity. Understanding how successful habit loops operate in these contexts can inspire individuals to create and sustain positive behaviors. Here are several notable examples of successful habit loops across different domains.

1. Health and Fitness: The Exercise Loop

One of the most well-documented examples of a successful habit loop is found in health and fitness routines. For many individuals, the habit loop surrounding exercise begins with a cue. This cue might be something as simple as the alarm clock going off in the morning or noticing workout clothes laid out the night before. The routine that follows this cue is the act of exercising, whether through running, attending a fitness class, or engaging in yoga. The reward could come in various forms: the rush of endorphins post-workout, the satisfaction of achieving fitness milestones, or tangible outcomes such as weight loss or improved strength.

The effectiveness of this habit loop is often amplified when individuals incorporate specific cues that align with their lifestyles. For instance, a person might leave their gym bag in the car as a visual prompt, reminding them to work out after work. By repeatedly engaging in this routine and experiencing the resulting physical and mental benefits, the habit of exercising becomes ingrained, ultimately leading to a more active lifestyle.

2. Professional Development: The Learning Loop

In the realm of professional development, successful habit loops can facilitate continuous learning and skill acquisition. For many professionals, the cue might be a specific day of the week or time of day set aside for personal development—such as Friday afternoons dedicated to professional reading or online courses. The routine involves engaging with learning materials, whether it be reading articles, watching webinars, or completing certification programs.

The reward for this habit loop can be immediate and long-term. The immediate gratification may come from increased knowledge and the sense of accomplishment derived from completing a course or mastering a new skill. In the long term, the enhancement of one's skill set can lead to career advancement opportunities and greater job satisfaction. By establishing a dedicated time for learning and fostering an environment conducive to professional development, individuals can create a robust learning habit that supports their career goals.

3. Cooking and Nutrition: The Meal Prep Loop

With the growing emphasis on healthy eating, the habit loop surrounding meal preparation has become increasingly popular. The cue in this scenario can often be a specific day of the week, like Sunday, designated for meal prep. Individuals may set aside this time to plan meals for the coming week, which serves as the initial trigger to kick-start the routine.

The routine involves selecting recipes, grocery shopping, and preparing meals in advance. The reward is multi-faceted; not only do individuals enjoy having healthy meals readily available throughout the week, but they also save time and reduce the stress of daily cooking. Additionally, the satisfaction of making healthy choices enhances feelings of accomplishment and well-being. This successful habit loop not only promotes better nutrition but also encourages creativity in cooking, thereby enhancing culinary skills over time.

4. Personal Finance: The Savings Loop

Another area where successful habit loops can thrive is in personal finance management. Many people adopt the "pay yourself first" principle as a cue to initiate their savings habit. This cue involves setting a specific day of the month—typically payday—when a predetermined amount of money is automatically transferred to a savings account. This actionable cue effectively initiates the savings routine.

The routine consists of adhering to a strict budget based on the remaining funds after savings have been deducted. The rewards associated with this habit loop can take various forms, such as the psychological boost from seeing savings accumulate, the preparation for future investments, or the peace of mind that comes with having a financial safety net. As individuals experience the benefits of their saving habits and recognize the power of compounded growth, their motivation to stick with the routine strengthens.

5. Mindfulness and Well-being: The Meditation Loop

Incorporating mindfulness practices into daily life can create powerful habit loops that enhance personal well-being. For individuals who practice meditation, the cue might be setting their morning alarm with a reminder to meditate or integrating it into their daily routine just before bedtime. The routine itself involves the act of meditation, which might include focused breathing, guided sessions, or mindfulness walks.

The rewards from this habit loop are significant. Many meditators report reduced stress levels, increased focus, and a greater sense of inner peace. The immediate feeling of relaxation after a session combined with the cumulative benefits of mindfulness leads to an increased desire to maintain the routine. Over time, as individuals observe profound shifts in their mental and emotional health, the meditation habit becomes a cherished and indispensable part of their lives.

6. Environmental Sustainability: The Recycling Loop

In the context of environmental sustainability, developing a habit loop around recycling can make a meaningful impact. The cue could be a designated recycling bin placed prominently in the home, serving as a daily reminder to recycle materials. The routine consists of sorting recyclable items from waste and actively engaging in recycling behaviors.

The reward demonstrates immediate gratification through the feeling of contributing positively to the environment, along with the long-term benefits of reducing waste and conserving resources. As individuals witness the impact of their actions—such as increased knowledge about environmental issues or participation in community clean-up efforts—the habit of recycling can deepen, encouraging not only personal responsibility but also community involvement.

7. Family and Relationships: The Connection Loop

Building and maintaining strong relationships requires intentional habits. A successful habit loop in this context might begin with a cue such as Saturday mornings that are set aside for family time. The routine that follows could involve engaging in activities together—like having a leisurely breakfast, going for a family hike, or participating in a game night.

The reward in this habit loop is the strengthening of family bonds, the creation of lasting memories, and the nurturing of open lines of communication. Over time, these intentional moments can create a resilient family culture and deepen connections among family members. The more consistently these moments are practiced, the more embedded the routine becomes within the family dynamic.

These examples illustrate how successful habit loops can operate across various contexts, enhancing the quality of life and facilitating personal growth. By understanding the cues, routines, and rewards that drive these loops, individuals can harness this knowledge to foster positive change in their own lives, regardless of the area in which they seek improvement.

Chapter 3: Identifying Your Habits

Identifying and assessing personal habits is a crucial step in the journey toward self-improvement. The awareness of our habits allows us to take the necessary steps to change detrimental behaviors and reinforce positive ones. The process of tracking and evaluating habits can be both enlightening and challenging, revealing patterns in our daily routines that might go unnoticed. Below, we will explore various methods to effectively track and assess your habits.

One of the simplest and most effective ways to start tracking your habits is through journaling. A habit journal serves as a personal record of your behaviors, thoughts, feelings, and the circumstances surrounding your habits. To begin, set aside a specific time each day to write about your activities, focusing particularly on your habits. You may want to document when and where a habit occurs, what triggered it, how you felt before and after engaging in the behavior, and any rewards you received. Over time, this reflective practice allows you to notice patterns, identify cues, and recognize the impacts of your habits on your overall well-being.

For individuals who prefer a more structured approach, habit-tracking apps can be a great alternative. These digital tools often come equipped with various features designed to help you monitor your behaviors over time. Many apps allow you to set specific goals and reminders, making it easier to stay accountable. They often provide visual graphs and statistics, highlighting your progress and patterns in your habits. Apps like Habitica, HabitBull, and Coach.me, for instance, offer unique interfaces that gamify the habit-tracking process, motivating you to stay committed to your goals. The convenience of having your habit tracker on your smartphone can facilitate consistency, ensuring that tracking becomes a part of your daily routine.

Another effective method for identifying and assessing your habits is the practice of self-assessment through the use of habit scorecards. A scorecard typically includes a list of habits you wish to track, divided into categories such as "positive" and "negative." Each day, you review your list and assign a score based on how well you adhered to your desired behaviors. You might use a simple scale from 1 to 5 or a more complex traffic light system where green indicates success, yellow indicates inconsistency, and red indicates failure. This visual representation can help you see trends over time, making it easier to pinpoint which habits require more attention and which are becoming ingrained.

Incorporating mindfulness techniques can also significantly enhance our ability to identify and assess habits. Mindfulness encourages us to observe our thoughts and behaviors without judgment, leading to a deeper understanding of why we engage in specific habits. By practicing mindfulness meditation, we can develop greater awareness of our habitual responses and emotional triggers. Keeping a mindfulness log, where you jot down insights gained during meditation or moments of heightened awareness throughout the day, can illuminate patterns that may have otherwise remained hidden.

Peer support and accountability can also prove invaluable in the habit-tracking process. Engaging with friends, family, or groups who share similar goals can create an environment of mutual encouragement and motivation. Consider forming a habit accountability group where members regularly share their progress, challenges, and achievements. Engaging in discussions about your assessment experiences fosters a sense of community and provides opportunities for feedback. Sometimes, simply sharing your goals verbally can help solidify your commitment to change.

When it comes to tracking specific types of habits, using clear metrics can lead to enhanced insight. For example, if you aim to improve your physical fitness, you could track details such as the duration and type of exercise, as well as how you feel post-workout. Similarly, if you're working to improve your diet, maintaining a food diary that includes your meals, portion sizes, and even emotional states during eating can reveal valuable connections between your habits and overall health. The key is to identify meaningful metrics pertinent to the habits you wish to modify and consistently monitor them.

Case studies of individuals who have successfully transformed their habits can also provide inspiration and guidance. Take, for instance, the story of John, who struggled with procrastination and poor time management. By diligently keeping a journal detailing his daily tasks, he uncovered general patterns that revealed specific times and activities where he was more likely to procrastinate. Armed with this data, he adjusted his schedule to prioritize important tasks during peak productivity hours and incorporated breaks strategically. John's reflection on his journaling enabled him to create a more balanced and effective routine, ultimately transforming his approach to work.

Another compelling case is that of Sarah, who set out to break her dependency on social media. By utilizing a habit-tracker app, she logged her daily screen time and noted when she felt the urge to check her phone. Over three weeks, Sarah noticed that the early evenings were her weakest moments for succumbing to this habit. With this knowledge, she decided to create a tech-free zone in her home during that time, thus allowing her to engage in more meaningful activities, such as reading and exercising. The application of tracking techniques not only helped her recognize her habit's cues but also empowered her to envision a lifestyle free from digital distractions.

Tracking and assessment of personal habits is a continuous journey that requires commitment and self-compassion. Whether through journaling, utilizing apps, employing mindfulness practices, or fostering supportive relationships, the methods for identifying and evaluating habits are abundant. What matters is finding the approach that resonates with you and is sustainable within your lifestyle. Every small step you take in this process contributes to a deeper understanding of yourself and, ultimately, guides you toward meaningful habit change. As you progress, remember that self-awareness is a powerful tool; it can illuminate the paths to positive transformation and enrich your life in profound ways.

In the process of exploring and understanding our habits, self-assessment is an essential component. Various tools can help us track, evaluate, and ultimately transform our habits into ones that serve us better. From traditional journaling methods to modern technological applications, the diversity of self-assessment tools allows individuals to find what resonates best with their personal style and needs. In this section, we will delve into several effective tools for self-assessment, including journaling, mobile apps, and other innovative techniques.

Journaling

Journaling is perhaps the most intimate and reflective method for tracking habits. This traditional tool not only helps document behaviors but also allows for deeper introspection about one's thoughts, feelings, and motivations. To begin journaling for habit tracking, set aside time daily or weekly to reflect on your behaviors. Consider keeping two types of journals: a habit-specific journal and a general reflective journal.

1. **Habit-specific Journal**: In this journal, you can list the particular habits you aim to track. Daily entries could include details such as:

- The specific habit being tracked

- Dates and times of engagement

- Triggers or cues that prompted the habit

- Emotional state before and after the habit

- Any rewards or consequences experienced

Over time, patterns may emerge, shedding light on when and why certain habits occur. This awareness is often the first step toward developing strategies for change.

2. **Reflective Journal**: A reflective journal serves a slightly different purpose.

In this, you can write about your thoughts and feelings related to your habits, the challenges you face, and any successes, no matter how small. You may also include insights gleaned from life events or external influences that impact your habits. The value of this journal lies in its capacity to help you process emotions and make connections between your habits and overall well-being.

Mobile Apps

With the proliferation of smartphones, habit-tracking apps have surged in popularity, presenting a convenient and efficient means to manage personal habits.

These digital tools often feature user-friendly interfaces that encourage consistent input and provide insights through data visualization. Here are several popular apps designed for habit tracking:

1. **Habitica**: This unique app gamifies habit tracking, allowing users to create a character that levels up by completing real-life tasks. By turning habit-forming into a game, Habitica motivates users through rewards and social interaction, making it an appealing choice for those who enjoy gaming elements.

2. **HabitBull**: HabitBull offers a highly customizable interface, enabling users to track multiple habits with various metrics. It provides charts and statistics to visualize progress and patterns, while reminders help users stay accountable. The flexibility of HabitBull caters to those who want to monitor habits ranging from daily exercise to reading more books.

3. **Streaks**: A visually appealing app, Streaks focuses on maintaining consecutive days of habit completion. Users can set their habits with clear metrics for tracking, and the app encourages users to keep their streak going, facilitating motivation through visual representation of progress.

4. **Coach.me**: This app functions as both a habit tracker and a coaching platform. Users can follow pre-set goals or customize their own, and they have access to a community of users and professional coaches for support and encouragement. The platform allows individuals to share their progress, adding a social element to habit tracking.

Using mobile apps not only makes tracking habits more straightforward but also cultivates immediacy and convenience, allowing users to log behaviors in real-time.

Other Methods of Self-Assessment

In addition to journaling and apps, there are other creative methods available for self-assessing habits that may better align with certain lifestyles or preferences.

1. **Bullet Journaling**: This method combines traditional journaling with planning, allowing users to create a customizable system for habit tracking. Bullet journals can include habit trackers, mood logs, and goal-setting pages, providing an all-in-one experience that encourages mindfulness about daily habits.

2. **Visual Habit Tracking**: Some individuals find that visual indicators, such as charts or infographics, help motivate them to maintain habits. This could involve drawing a habit tracker on paper or creating an art piece that represents your habits' progress visually. Some people even opt for sticker charts, where they earn stickers for each day they complete a habit.

3. **Mind Mapping**: Mind mapping is a brainstorming method that visualizes relationships between different ideas. You can create a mind map centered around one habit, branching out to explore its triggers, feelings associated with it, and potential areas for improvement. This exercise can provide insight into the broader context of a habit and how to approach it.

4. **Audio Journaling**: For those who prefer verbal expression over written words, audio journaling is a fantastic alternative. Recording your thoughts about your habits, daily successes, and challenges using a voice memo app can be an engaging experience. Listening back allows for retrospective insights, making it easier to identify patterns over time.

5. **Accountability Partners**: Having an accountability partner can provide immense motivation in tracking habits. This method involves sharing your goals with someone you trust, who can check in with you regularly. You can discuss progress and struggles, providing mutual support that can bolster commitment to

both parties. This social element often enhances the effectiveness of self-assessment.

6. **Checklists**: A straightforward yet effective way to assess habits is through the use of checklists. By creating a list of habits you wish to track, you can simply mark off completion each day. This tangible method provides clear visual acknowledgment of progress, offering a sense of accomplishment.

7. **Weekly or Monthly Review Sessions**: Allocate time at the end of each week or month to review your habit-tracking efforts. During this time, reflect on what went well and what didn't, analyze the patterns you've noticed, and reassess your approach moving forward. This practice of reflection solidifies lessons learned and encourages growth.

Case Studies of Individuals Transforming Their Habits

To illustrate the transformative power of habit identification and modification, let's delve into several real-life case studies that showcase how individuals have reshaped their habits and, consequently, their lives.

Case Study 1: Jane's Journey to Health

Jane, a 34-year-old marketing professional, struggled for years with unhealthy eating habits and a sedentary lifestyle. Her routine consisted of grabbing fast food for lunch and binge-watching television in the evenings. After undergoing a health scare that prompted her to visit a doctor, Jane realized she needed to make significant lifestyle changes to improve her well-being.

Determined to change, Jane started by tracking her eating habits and physical activity through a journaling app. Each day, she logged what she ate, along with the time and her mood at the time of eating. This self-assessment helped her identify two critical patterns: she often snacked mindlessly while watching TV and turned to fast food when feeling stressed.

With this newfound awareness, Jane implemented gradual changes. She began meal prepping on Sundays to avoid last-minute food decisions during the week. By preparing healthy, balanced meals in advance, Jane found herself less reliant on fast food. Moreover, she replaced her evening TV binges with short, two-minute workouts, another technique she learned about from her habit research.

This initial commitment to two-minute workouts helped her build momentum, and soon, those two minutes turned into thirty-minute exercise sessions. Over several months, Jane lost weight, increased her energy levels, and felt a newfound sense of control over her life. By actively recognizing her bad habits and replacing them with healthier ones, Jane transformed her entire lifestyle.

Case Study 2: Mark's Financial Turnaround

Mark, a 45-year-old software engineer, found himself drowning in debt. Despite earning a decent salary, he had developed a habit of impulsive spending, especially when it came to online shopping. Feeling overwhelmed, Mark decided to take a systematic approach to understand his financial habits.

To begin, Mark tracked his spending habits using a financial management app that allowed him to categorize each purchase. At the end of each week, he reviewed his spending patterns and noted down recurring themes—he discovered that he often impulsively bought items when feeling bored or stressed after work.

With this insight, Mark developed a plan to curb his impulse purchases. First, he set a budget for discretionary spending and vowed to limit those expenses for a month. This required him to find alternative activities to address his boredom, such as engaging in hobbies he let slip over the years.

Mark also implemented a 24-hour rule for non-essential purchases, giving him time to reflect on whether he truly needed an item before buying it. By the month's end, he noticed that his spending had significantly decreased, and with the money saved, he started building an emergency fund.

Mark's experience showcases how self-assessment not only helps in recognizing negative habits but also equips individuals with the tools to replace them with financially wise behaviors. Gradually, he transformed his relationship with money, leading to a more secure financial future.

Case Study 3: Sarah's Inward Journey

Sarah, a 28-year-old teacher, found herself plagued by a cycle of self-doubt and procrastination. This often impacted her professional responsibilities and left her feeling unfulfilled. To combat these feelings, she turned to journaling, a tool suggested by a close friend.

In her journal, Sarah began to track her daily accomplishments, no matter how small, and identify the triggers that led to her procrastination. She realized that she often delayed important tasks because of a paralyzing fear of failure.

This self-exploration led Sarah to seek professional help, where she learned about cognitive behavioral strategies to replace negative thoughts with positive affirmations. Over time, she established a morning routine that included gratitude journaling, mindfulness meditation, and setting daily intentions.

By cultivating these new habits and actively reframing her thought patterns, Sarah began to feel more confident in her abilities. Her willingness to confront her struggles head-on resulted in increased productivity, enhanced relationships with colleagues, and an overall sense of joy in her career.

Sarah's journey illustrates the profound impact that tracking habits can have on personal growth and self-improvement. By fostering a continuous dialogue with herself through journaling, she was able to break the cycle of procrastination and build a more fulfilling life.

Case Study 4: Tom's Quest for Mindfulness

Tom, a 39-year-old executive, faced high levels of stress and anxiety due to the demands of his job. He often resorted to distractions, such as scrolling through social media, to escape from stress. Recognizing this behavior as unproductive, Tom began his quest for mindfulness.

He first utilized a mindfulness app to track his meditation and mindfulness practices. The app provided him with guided sessions, allowing him to start with just a few minutes each day. Tom documented his thoughts and feelings before and after each session, enabling him to better understand the benefits of these practices and track his progress.

Within weeks, Tom noticed a significant change in his ability to cope with stress. The regular practice of mindfulness allowed him to break the habit of reaching for his phone as a distraction. Instead, he would take a few deep breaths or simply sit in silence for a couple of minutes when feeling overwhelmed.

As Tom continued his practice, he also became more intentional about how he spent his time outside of work. He replaced some of his evening screen time with books, nature walks, and quality moments with family. Tom's transformation not only reduced his anxiety but also improved his focus, productivity, and overall happiness.

These case studies illustrate the diverse ways individuals have successfully identified and transformed their habits. Each person's journey underscores the importance of self-awareness, the use of assessment tools, and the commitment to making gradual changes. By embracing new patterns and practices, these individuals have empowered themselves to live healthier, more fulfilling lives, reminding us all of the potential that lies in understanding and reshaping our habits.

** Chapter 4: Building New Habits **

When it comes to creating new, positive habits, a variety of strategies can help ensure success. These strategies are not one-size-fits-all; they need to be personalized to fit individual lifestyles and preferences. However, there are fundamental principles that can guide anyone looking to establish new routines that enhance their wellbeing and productivity.

1. Start Small and Specific

One of the most effective strategies for habit formation is to start with small, specific actions. Instead of overwhelming yourself with grand gestures or vague goals, break down your desired habit into manageable tasks. For instance, if your aim is to cultivate a habit of reading, rather than committing to read a book every week, start with a goal of reading just a page each day. This specificity provides clarity and makes the task less daunting. Over time, as you build confidence and consistency, you can gradually increase your targets.

2. Utilize the "Two-Minute Rule"

A well-known springboard for establishing new habits is the "two-minute rule."

This concept, popularized by productivity expert James Clear, suggests that any new habit should take less than two minutes to complete initially. The rationale behind this approach is that it lowers the barrier to entry, making it easier to start. If you want to develop a habit of running, for instance, commit to putting on your running shoes and stepping outside for just two minutes. This small start can lead to longer sessions as you become accustomed to the routine. The key is that the initial commitment is so minimal that it becomes almost effortless to engage in. I will talk about this in more detail in the next section.

3. Identify Your Cues

To establish a new habit, it's essential to identify and leverage cues that trigger the desired behavior. Cues can be external, such as time of day or physical environments, or internal, like emotions or feelings. By associating your new habit with a specific cue, you can create a reliable trigger that reminds you to perform the routine. For example, if your goal is to practice mindfulness each day, you could choose to meditate right after brushing your teeth every morning. The act of brushing your teeth becomes the cue that initiates your mindfulness practice.

4. Create a Supportive Environment

Your environment plays a critical role in habit formation. By designing a space that supports your new habits, you make it easier to stick to them. For example, if you're trying to eat healthier, keeping fresh fruits and vegetables visible and accessible on your kitchen counter can serve as a daily reminder to make better food choices. Conversely, removing temptations—such as hiding unhealthy snacks—can help reduce the likelihood of slipping into old habits. Additionally, surrounding yourself with individuals who embody the habits you wish to adopt can serve as inspiration and accountability.

5. Establish Clear Rewards

Rewarding yourself after successfully completing your habit can help solidify the behavior in your routine. Ensure that the rewards align with your overall goals; they should reinforce the positive changes you're trying to implement. For instance, if your goal is to exercise regularly, a satisfying reward might be taking a relaxing bath or enjoying a favorite snack after a workout. The reward creates a positive association with your new habit, making it more likely that you'll continue the behavior in the long term.

6. Track Your Progress

Monitoring your progress is vital in maintaining motivation and a sense of accomplishment. Keeping a record of your new habits not only allows you to observe how consistent you are but can also highlight trends, such as peak times when you're more likely to stick to your routines. This could be as simple as using a habit tracking app, marking a calendar, or maintaining a journal. The act of tracking can serve as a powerful motivator, and seeing your progress can encourage you to keep pushing forward.

7. Reframe Your Mindset

Cultivating a positive mindset regarding your new habits is crucial. If you approach habit formation with the belief that you "have" to do it, it may feel more like a chore than a choice. Instead, reframe your thoughts to view habits as opportunities for growth and self-improvement. Focus on the benefits and personal values aligned with these habits. For example, if your goal is to meditate daily, think of it not as a task to check off, but as a precious time you're gifting yourself for mental clarity and peace.

8. Be Patient and Forgiving

Habit formation is a journey that requires patience. It's important to acknowledge that progress may be slow, and setbacks can occur. Instead of being overly critical of yourself for lapses, practice self-compassion. Understand that building a new habit is a gradual process, and even if you miss a day or two, it doesn't mean you've failed. Reflect on what led to the deviation and how you can adjust your approach moving forward. Cultivating resilience will empower you to persist, even when it feels challenging.

9. Leverage Social Accountability

Sharing your goals with others can significantly enhance your chances of success. This could involve telling friends, family, or colleagues about the habit you're trying to establish or even joining a community or group with similar aspirations. Social accountability creates a sense of obligation and support, making it harder to give up on your commitments. Regular check-ins or shared experiences can provide encouragement and inspiration, reminding you that you are not alone in your journey.

10. Embrace Flexibility and Adaptation

Finally, understand that building new habits is not a rigid process. It's essential to remain flexible and willing to adapt your approach as necessary. Life circumstances may change, and what worked for you in one phase might not suit another. Be open to experimenting with different strategies and adjusting your goals as you evolve. Embracing this fluidity allows you to find what truly works for you and helps you maintain motivation over the long term.

By applying these strategies thoughtfully and consistently, you can lay the foundation for lasting, positive habits that will enhance your overall quality of life. Remember, the journey of habit formation is not just about the end goal; it's about the growth and insights gained along the way.

The Role of Small Changes and Incremental Progress (the "2-Minute Rule")

The journey of building new habits often begins with a single, small step—an insight that the "2-minute rule" encapsulates beautifully. This powerful concept emphasizes the importance of starting small, making the habit formation process feel approachable and achievable.

Understanding the 2-Minute Rule

The essence of the 2-minute rule is simple: when you want to establish a new habit, find a way to make it take less than two minutes to start. This technique effectively reduces resistance and lowers the psychological barriers that often prevent individuals from taking action. When a task feels quick and manageable, it is significantly easier to initiate, paving the way for longer commitments over time.

James Clear, in his book "Atomic Habits," discusses the notion of "starting with something easy" as a fundamental principle for habit formation. The idea is that by focusing on small, doable actions, you set yourself up for success rather than overwhelming yourself with lofty expectations from the outset.

The Power of Small Steps

Incremental changes can yield profound results over time. Consider someone looking to develop a fitness routine. Instead of setting a goal to spend an hour at the gym every day, the individual might commit to doing just two minutes of exercise at home—be it stretching, push-ups, or even a few jumping jacks. These small victories are vital because they encourage the individual to begin the practice without the pressure of a larger commitment.

As individuals repeatedly engage in these small actions, they can often discover that the initial two minutes naturally extend. In many cases, once someone gets moving, they are likely to continue for longer than originally intended—this is the trigger effect. The act of just starting creates momentum, leading to the establishment of a more sustained practice.

Building Momentum and Confidence

One of the psychological benefits of the 2-minute rule is the sense of accomplishment it fosters. Completing a small task can trigger the release of dopamine—a neurotransmitter associated with feelings of satisfaction and pleasure. This "reward" reinforces the new behavior and can create a positive feedback loop.

When you set out to accomplish something that feels manageable, you experience immediate success, which builds confidence. Over time, these small wins accumulate, leading to greater commitment and ultimately enabling you to tackle more ambitious goals as your habit solidifies.

For example, someone who starts by reading just one page a day might find that once they open the book and read the first page, they naturally continue for another few pages or even an entire chapter. This incremental approach not only promotes resilience but also nurtures a positive, growth-focused mindset in the habit formation process.

Strategies to Implement the 2-Minute Rule

To effectively implement the 2-minute rule in your daily life, consider the following strategies:

1. **Identify Your Goals**: Define what new habits you wish to cultivate and ensure they align with your broader aspirations. This clarity will help in determining appropriate 2-minute actions.

2. **Break Down Habits**: Deconstruct your desired habit into its most basic form. Ask yourself, "What is the smallest version of this habit that I can commit to?" List the actions that can be completed in two minutes or less.

3. **Schedule Your Mini-Habits**: Incorporate these 2-minute tasks into your daily schedule. Consider utilizing specific times of the day when you are most likely to engage, such as first thing in the morning or during a lunch break. Build them into your routine seamlessly.

4. **Set Up Reminders**: Use reminders or cues to prompt you to perform your mini-habit. Whether it's an alarm on your phone or sticky notes placed strategically around your home, these nudges are critical for maintaining visibility and accountability.

5. **Celebrate Small Wins**: Acknowledge and celebrate your commitment to the 2-minute actions, even if they seem insignificant at first! This recognition reinforces positive behavior and motivates you to continue.

6. **Gradually Build Up**: Once you have solidified your ability to perform the mini-habit, gradually increase the duration or complexity. After consistently completing two minutes of exercise, aim for five minutes, and then eventually extend it to longer sessions.

Transformative Impacts of Incremental Change

The significance of the 2-minute rule transcends individual habits—it speaks to a broader philosophy of progress and development. In an age where instant gratification often overshadows the value of sustained effort, recognizing the power of small changes becomes essential for long-term success.

Incremental change promotes a healthier relationship with personal development. Instead of overwhelming ourselves with impossible transformations, we can embrace the slow but steady process of consistent improvement. This reframing of success allows individuals to bypass feelings of defeat that sometimes accompany major life changes, establishing a sustainable pattern of growth.

Furthermore, small changes resonate at a deeper level psychologically. When individuals engage in consistent, bite-sized habits, they align themselves with the idea of identity change—shifting their self-perception over time. Someone who reads for two minutes daily gradually begins to see themselves as a reader, which can influence their willingness to devote time to reading longer and more often in the future.

The Role of Context and Environment

The effectiveness of the 2-minute rule can also be enhanced by considering the context in which you are attempting to build your new habit. By adjusting your environment to make it easier to engage in these micro-habits, you can further reduce any forms of friction that might otherwise deter you.

For instance, if your goal is to meditate daily, setting up a dedicated meditation space with cushions and calming scents can serve as a visual reminder for your practice. This environment signifies readiness and intention, creating a more conducive setting for beginning your two-minute meditation sessions.

Additionally, anchoring your new mini-habits to existing daily routines can also facilitate easier formation. For example, if you consistently brush your teeth every morning, follow it up with two minutes of stretching. By closely tying your new habit to a well-established behavior, you create a natural opportunity for practice.

As you progress through the journey of building new habits using the 2-minute rule, remember that patience and persistence are integral components of sustained success. Recognize that significant transformations don't occur overnight; instead, they manifest over days, weeks, and months through consistent, incremental efforts.

By embracing the inherent nature of small progress, you align yourself with a more compassionate and realistic view of self-improvement. This perspective encourages long-term commitment and resilience, allowing you to navigate challenges and setbacks without becoming disheartened.

Through the lens of the 2-minute rule, the path to building new habits becomes one of empowerment rather than obligation. When faced with the daunting task of cultivating change, remember that each small step brings you closer to the person you aspire to be, and over time, these small, consistent actions will yield remarkable results.

The Importance of Consistency and Patience

As we delve deeper into the process of building new habits, the significance of consistency and patience cannot be overstated. These two elements serve as the bedrock upon which successful habit formation is constructed. In a world that often prioritizes quick fixes and immediate results, it's essential to recognize that meaningful change typically unfolds over time. Developing a new habit is not merely about a single action or a transient burst of motivation; it demands a sustained commitment to repetition and gradual improvement.

Consistency entails regularly engaging in the desired behavior, day after day, regardless of external circumstances or internal fluctuations in motivation. It's this regularity that solidifies behaviors into habits. When we think of consistent action, we might envision someone waking up at the same time each morning, practicing a musical instrument daily, or exercising on a regular schedule. These commitments reinforce the habit through repeated practice, allowing the brain to encode the behavior as a default mode. The neurological pathways strengthened by consistency make it easier over time to initiate the action without relying heavily on conscious effort or willpower.

Furthermore, consistent effort creates a sense of momentum. Just as a train takes time to build speed, our habits require a similar gradual buildup. With each day that a new behavior is practiced, the likelihood of it becoming ingrained increases. This momentum can be motivating, as we begin to experience the cumulative effects of our efforts. Positive reinforcement may also arise—the satisfaction of completing our goal, improvements in our skills, or benefits such as increased health or productivity serve to encourage us to maintain our routine.

Patience, conversely, is the quality that allows us to endure the process of habit formation without becoming disheartened by a lack of immediate results. In our fast-paced society, it's easy to fall prey to the belief that quick rewards are the only measures of success. When building new habits, however, it is crucial to approach the journey with the understanding that mastery comes over time. This means acknowledging that there may be days when motivation wanes or when setbacks occur. Patience equips us with the resilience needed to navigate these obstacles constructively.

Approaching habit formation with patience also requires an appreciation for the small wins on the path to larger goals. It's essential to recognize that every single action, no matter how minor it may seem, contributes to the overall progress. For instance, if your goal is to read more books, reading a mere two pages each day may not feel substantial at first. However, by consistently engaging with this small activity, you can find yourself finishing numerous books over the course of a year—a reflection of the power of incremental improvement.

Moreover, cultivating habits that stick takes time because our brains are inherently wired to prefer comfort and familiarity. The initial phase of trying to form new habits often feels uncomfortable as we challenge the status quo of our routines. During this period, doubt may creep in, leading to the temptation of abandoning the effort altogether. Practicing patience encourages us to persist through this discomfort, as it empowers us to trust the process rather than succumb to discouragement.

Another facet of patience is the acceptance of our imperfections as part of the journey. It is rare for habit formation to be a linear progression. There will be days when we miss our target or feel overwhelmed, but patience reminds us that these slips are not failures; they are part of the learning curve. Understanding this, we can view setbacks as opportunities to reflect on our strategies and adjust our approach rather than as signs of inadequacy. Each missed day can serve as a learning experience, helping us identify challenges and develop strategies for overcoming them in the future.

Equally important is the realization that the benefits of new habits may not be immediately evident. For example, if you start exercising regularly, it may take weeks or months to notice changes in your body or feel significant improvements in your energy levels. During this period, maintaining consistency becomes paramount, as it is the repeated action that sets the foundation for eventual results. Cultivating patience allows you to stay the course, even when progress seems slow, thereby keeping the vision of long-term reward alive.

Moreover, embedding new habits into our daily routine can lead to shifts in identity and self-perception over time. As we repeatedly engage in positive behaviors, we may begin to see ourselves as healthy individuals, committed learners, or dedicated professionals. This evolution in self-view reinforces our commitment to the habit and encourages us to keep going, as we align our actions with our emerging identity. The patience to foster this transformation is crucial; it unfolds gradually as our new behaviors crystallize into our self-image.

In the context of community and support, patience enhances our ability to navigate social dynamics around habit formation. Seeking encouragement from friends, family, or peer groups often fosters accountability and camaraderie. However, these relationships also require time to develop, as trust and understanding grow through shared experiences. Through consistent efforts, we foster connections that support our growth and provide a network of encouragement, especially on tough days. The reciprocal nature of these relationships highlights the value of patience, as we learn to rely on one another's strengths as we strive towards our individual goals.

Ultimately, the confluence of consistency and patience creates a powerful framework for sustainable change. It cultivates a mindset that values long-term success over fleeting gratification, allowing us to create a resilient foundation for habit formation. By embracing both consistency in our actions and patience in our progress, we lay the groundwork for new habits to flourish over time, transforming our intentions into lasting behaviors that define our lives.

Chapter 5: Breaking Bad Habits

One of the most daunting challenges we face on the journey toward self-improvement is breaking free from negative habits. These behaviors, often ingrained and automatic, can feel insurmountable at times. However, the first step in overcoming them is recognizing their presence in our lives. This awareness is crucial because without acknowledging a habit, it becomes exceedingly difficult to alter or eliminate it. Techniques for recognizing and eliminating these negative habits can be transformative, paving the way for a more positive future.

The process of identification begins with self-reflection and mindfulness. Setting aside time for introspection allows us to examine our daily routines and behaviors critically. Keeping a journal can be particularly helpful in this stage. By documenting our actions throughout the day, we can highlight patterns—what we do, when we do it, and in response to what triggers. Over time, these entries can provide valuable insight into habits we may not have recognized as detrimental. For example, we might find we consistently reach for snacks when we feel stressed, revealing a habit of emotional eating that we need to address.

Another useful approach is to gather feedback from trusted friends or family members. Often, those who are close to us can identify behaviors that we might overlook. Engaging in open conversations about our habits can yield eye-opening revelations. They may notice patterns, such as our tendency to procrastinate or withdraw in social situations, that we may be blind to. This external perspective can be instrumental in the recognition process, as it can give us the nudge we need to confront the habits we'd rather ignore.

Once we have identified our negative habits, we must examine the underlying cues and rewards that maintain them. Using the "habit loop" framework—cue, routine, reward—we can dissect our patterns further. By asking ourselves what triggers a negative behavior, we can begin to understand its context. Is it stress that leads to binge-watching television instead of working on a project? Is it boredom that drives the desire to scroll endlessly through social media? Recognizing these cues is crucial because they often serve as gateways to engaging in the routine we aim to change.

With an understanding of cues in place, we can then turn our focus to the routine aspect of our habits. This step involves reflecting on whether the routine delivers a genuine reward. Many bad habits thrive on the illusion of satisfaction, offering a fleeting sense of comfort or relief that quickly dissipates. For instance, while smoking may provide temporary stress relief, it ultimately leads to health issues and a cycle of dependence. Thus, it's essential to dissect not just what we do, but why we do it. This understanding can foster motivation for change; if we can find healthier alternatives that provide similar rewards, we may find it easier to relinquish our bad habits.

Through awareness of cues, routines, and rewards, we can start strategizing ways to disrupt the cycle. One effective technique is to implement "implementation intentions," a psychological strategy that involves planning specific responses to certain cues. For example, if you recognize that checking social media is a habit triggered when you sit down at your computer, you might set an intention such as, "When I sit down to work, I will open a productivity app instead." By formulating clear plans for how to respond to cues, we create a framework for replacing bad behaviors with healthier ones.

Another valuable tool is environmental modification. Our environments significantly influence our habits, and by reshaping them, we can either reinforce or break existing patterns. For example, if snacking while watching television is a negative habit, one strategy could be to change the environment. Instead of having snacks readily available in the kitchen, stash them in an out-of-reach cabinet or eliminate them altogether. Creating a space that minimizes exposure to cues can also aid in breaking the cycle. This might involve removing distractions from your workspace to enhance focus or altering your route to avoid habitual stops for unhealthy food.

Peer accountability can also dramatically facilitate acknowledgment and change of bad habits. Being part of a group striving for similar goals can mitigate feelings of isolation and increase motivation. Joining a support group or finding an accountability partner allows for shared experiences and encouragement. Regular check-ins with someone who understands our goals can provide the necessary reinforcement to stay committed to breaking bad habits. This approach taps into the power of community, reminding us that we are not alone in our struggles.

In addition to seeking support from others, it is vital to cultivate self-compassion throughout the process. Breaking bad habits is often messy and nonlinear, with setbacks along the way. Embracing a mindset of kindness toward ourselves can mitigate feelings of shame or defeat that arise from temporary failures. Recognizing that habits are built over time allows for the grace needed to navigate setbacks without derailing the entire process. Instead of viewing a slip as a definitive end, we can learn from it and reinforce our renewed commitment to change.

At the heart of breaking bad habits is the understanding that replacement is often more effective than outright elimination. Instead of solely focusing on stopping a negative behavior, we should direct our efforts toward finding constructive alternatives. This means identifying activities that fulfill the same needs as the habit we want to break. For instance, if stress eating is a problem, replacing the habit with a healthier outlet such as going for a walk or practicing meditation can be beneficial. Engaging in physical activity not only distracts us from the urge to snack but also provides a natural stress reliever, contributing positively to our overall health.

By utilizing these techniques for recognizing and eliminating negative habits, we grant ourselves the power to take deliberate actions toward creating a healthier future. Self-reflection, feedback, environmental changes, and supportive social networks are all integral components of this journey. As we work to identify and replace behaviors that no longer serve us, we open doors to new possibilities, allowing for growth and transformation as we step into a more positive version of ourselves.

As we navigate the complex terrain of breaking bad habits, the role of accountability and social support emerges as a critical factor in ensuring our success. While the journey of personal change often feels solitary, seeking support from others can significantly enhance our motivation, commitment, and resilience. This section delves into how accountability and social networks can serve as powerful allies in the quest to eliminate negative habits, shaping our behaviors and reinforcing our resolve.

Accountability, at its core, involves establishing commitments to ourselves or others that keep us in check. This practice transcends mere willpower; it introduces an external layer of responsibility that can enhance our self-discipline. When we articulate our goals to others, we are more likely to follow through on them. The simple act of vocalizing an intention creates a sense of obligation, prompting us to align our actions with our declared objectives. For instance, if you share your goal of quitting smoking with a friend or family member, their awareness of your commitment can serve as a reminder when you are tempted to revert to your old ways.

Accountability partnerships can be established in various forms. One of the most effective avenues is aligning with someone who shares a common goal or a similar challenge. For example, if you're looking to break the habit of excessive screen time, finding a friend who is also trying to limit their device usage creates a mutual support system. You can regularly check in with each other, share progress, and offer encouragement. This shared journey fosters an environment of understanding and empathy, making the process less daunting.

Beyond personal partnerships, accountability can also flourish in the context of structured groups or support networks. Joining a support group provides a platform where individuals come together to share experiences and wisdom. Whether through in-person meetings or online communities, engaging with others who are on similar journeys can offer a sense of belonging. Here, individuals can voice their struggles, celebrate their victories, and glean insights from diverse perspectives. Groups, such as those focused on quitting smoking or adopting healthier lifestyles, embody this principle, reminding us that we are not alone in our struggles.

An additional aspect to consider is the role of technology in facilitating accountability. Mobile applications designed for habit tracking or goal setting can serve as modern tools to record progress and manage behaviors. Many of these applications incorporate community features that allow users to connect, share experiences, and support one another through the process. By receiving notifications or reminders from these tools, individuals reinforce their commitment to change while fostering a sense of connection with others striving for similar goals.

The emotional support found in accountability relationships cannot be underestimated. On tough days, when motivation wanes and temptations loom larger, having someone to reach out to can make all the difference. A supportive friend or family member can provide encouragement and serve as a critical sounding board. They can help you reframe setbacks, reminding you to view them as temporary obstacles rather than insurmountable barriers. This perspective shift can be empowering, allowing individuals to maintain their momentum despite challenges.

Moreover, sharing progress and celebrating achievements, no matter how small, can significantly bolster our motivation. When we experience and vocalize success—such as completing a full week without engaging in a negative behavior—we reinforce our commitment to continued improvement. Our accountability partners can help us acknowledge these milestones, promoting a positive feedback loop that fuels our determination to persist. Recognition from others can provide reassurance and validation that our efforts are worthwhile, reinforcing the notion that change is possible.

However, it's essential to note that not all social interactions are equally beneficial. Surrounding ourselves with individuals who are supportive and encouraging is paramount. Conversely, engaging with those who might inadvertently reinforce negative habits can be counterproductive. Therefore, an honest assessment of our social circles may be necessary. We must seek out and nourish relationships that inspire us to grow, challenge us to stay committed, and offer constructive feedback without judgment.

In some cases, it may be beneficial to share our goals with a broader audience, such as through social media platforms or community forums. Posting updates about our progress can create a sense of accountability to a wider audience, providing an additional layer of support. This public declaration can attract encouragement from unexpected sources, creating a network of support that extends beyond our immediate circle. However, it is essential to approach this with care; while positive reinforcement can be motivating, negative feedback can be discouraging. Therefore, choosing the right platforms and communities that foster constructive dialogue becomes essential.

As we harness the power of accountability in breaking bad habits, we should also remember the importance of reciprocal support. Supporting others in their efforts can deepen our commitment to our goals as well. When we lend our ears to a friend struggling with their own habits, we cultivate a sense of empathy that reinforces our desire for self-improvement. The act of being accountable toward others often inspires us to stay true to our commitments as we become aware of our mutual reliance.

In conclusion, incorporating accountability and social support into our journey of breaking bad habits offers a robust framework for change. The influence of others—be it through personal relationships, support groups, or digital platforms—can bolster our resolve and facilitate our progress. By fostering connections that inspire and uplift, we create an environment in which transformation is possible. Through these supportive dynamics, we can reshape our behaviors and pave the way toward a healthier, more fulfilling life.

Finding alternatives and replacing bad habits with healthier options is a pivotal strategy in the journey toward personal transformation. While eliminating negative habits is important, simply ceasing a behavior often leaves a void that can lead to feelings of restlessness or frustration. To build lasting change, it is crucial to identify positive behaviors that fulfill similar functions. This section explores effective strategies for replacing detrimental habits with healthier alternatives, ensuring not just cessation but a holistic improvement in lifestyle.

The first step in this process is understanding the underlying reasons for a habit's existence—what needs it fulfills in our lives. Often, habits develop as coping mechanisms for stress, boredom, or emotional pain. For instance, excessive snacking might arise from emotional stress or a need for comfort, while procrastination may stem from fear or anxiety about a task. By understanding the triggers that lead to these behaviors, we can begin to search for alternatives that satisfy the same needs but contribute positively to our well-being.

Identifying healthier alternatives requires a bit of creativity and self-awareness. It can be helpful to brainstorm a list of activities that provide similar rewards to the negative behaviors we wish to replace. Take, for example, the habit of sitting on the couch and binge-watching television for hours. If the motivation stems from a need to unwind and relax, alternatives could include engaging in a captivating book, practicing yoga, or taking a leisurely walk in nature. The objective is to find substitutes that not only fulfill the need for relaxation but also enhance our physical or mental health in the process.

Another approach involves the use of "replacement behaviors." Instead of seeing habit-breaking as a series of "nos," reframing it to include "yeses" can provide a more positive perspective. For example, if you are trying to quit smoking, replace the action of smoking with something that occupies your hands and mouth, such as chewing gum or using a stress ball. This not only distracts you from the urge to smoke but also aids in managing the physical sensations associated with the habit. Similarly, recognizing the cue for smoking may lead to substituting the routine of stepping outside for a cigarette with a five-minute stretch or a few deep breathing exercises.

Engaging in physical activity is one powerful alternative that can fill the void left by many bad habits. Exercise serves a dual purpose: it not only distracts from urges but also releases endorphins, which naturally elevate our mood. If the urge to engage in a negative behavior arises, such as late-night snacking or excessive scrolling through social media, taking a quick walk, doing a few stretches, or even hitting the gym can redirect that energy into something positive. Over time, this shift can contribute to improved physical fitness, boosted confidence, and a greater sense of accomplishment.

The process of replacing bad habits also entails making gradual adjustments rather than abrupt changes. Small, incremental shifts can be more sustainable compared to drastic alterations that may feel overwhelming. For instance, if aiming to reduce soda consumption, one could start by substituting half of the soda intake with flavored sparkling water rather than quitting soda cold turkey. This stepwise approach not only eases the transition but also allows for the gradual development of new, healthier preferences over time.

Mindfulness practices can also be an effective tool for replacing harmful habits. Often, bad habits are executed automatically, without conscious thought. By cultivating mindfulness, we increase awareness of our actions and triggers. Techniques such as meditation, deep breathing, or simply pausing to reflect before acting can help create a space between impulse and action. This moment of reflection allows for the evaluation of what alternative behaviors might be more beneficial in the moment. For example, when the urge to mindlessly scroll through social media arises, a moment of mindfulness can encourage a switch to a short, calming meditation instead.

Social support plays a crucial role here as well—engaging your support system can provide suggestions for alternative behaviors. Friends and family might introduce new activities, hobbies, or interests that can replace unwelcome habits. For instance, instead of meeting for unhealthy snacks and drinks, a friend might suggest a day of hiking or cooking a healthy meal together. The more aligned our interactions are with our goals for positive change, the more likely we are to succeed in forming new habits.

Finding meaningful alternatives can also involve getting involved in activities that build skills or exploring new passions. Hobbies such as painting, knitting, gardening, or playing a musical instrument not only provide a fulfilling alternative to time spent in negative habits but also foster creativity and personal growth. As we immerse ourselves in fulfilling activities, we occupy our time with pursuits that enhance our lives and draw our attention away from harmful habits. Investing time in learning and growth can also contribute to a stronger sense of purpose and fulfillment, reducing the desire for escapism through negative behaviors.

In addition to adopting healthier alternatives, it is vital to create an environment conducive to change. Surrounding ourselves with positive stimuli that encourage our new habits can make a significant difference. For instance, if working to replace television time with reading, placing books in easily accessible areas serves as a physical reminder of the new goal. Similarly, if we endeavor to cook healthy meals instead of opting for takeout, keeping fresh produce visible in our kitchens and removing unhealthy snacks from sight can reduce the temptation to revert to old habits.

It's also essential to acknowledge that setbacks are part of the journey. Finding alternatives and replacing bad habits is not a linear process; it involves experimentation and embracing a trial-and-error mentality. Some alternatives may resonate more than others, and becoming comfortable with adjusting our strategies is essential. Be generous with yourself during this process—celebrating small victories and learning from missteps is what ultimately propels us forward.

In summary, the quest to find alternatives and replace bad habits with healthier options is a multifaceted approach that encompasses self-awareness, creativity, and a support system. By understanding the needs that our bad habits fulfill, we can identify and implement positive replacements that not only help us eliminate destructive behaviors but also enhance our overall quality of life. Through a combination of mindful reflection, gradual changes, and meaningful engagement, we can navigate the path to personal growth and transformation, enriching our lives in the process.

**Chapter 6: The Power of Environment **

The world around us is a powerful facilitator of our actions and choices, shaping the intricate web of our daily habits. From the physical spaces we inhabit to the people we interact with, our environment plays a crucial role in habit formation, often more than we realize. Understanding this influence can equip us to make conscious decisions about the settings we choose to create, enhancing our ability to cultivate positive habits and diminish detrimental ones.

To begin with, let's explore the physical environment—our homes, workplaces, and public spaces. The arrangement of our surroundings can significantly impact our behaviors. For instance, a cluttered desk can lead to feelings of overwhelm, making it more challenging to focus on tasks and, as a result, hindering productivity. In contrast, an organized and aesthetically pleasing workspace often promotes a sense of calm and efficiency, encouraging better work habits. Thus, by intentionally designing our environments to minimize distractions and promote focus, we can pave the way for more effective habit formation.

Consider also the simple yet profound principle of visibility. A common strategy in habit development advocates for making cues for desired behaviors more visible. For example, placing healthy snacks in clear view rather than hiding them in the pantry can significantly influence dietary choices. The act of seeing those snacks serves as a reminder to make a healthier choice, reinforcing that habit. Conversely, if we wish to break a habit—like excessive screen time—hiding devices out of sight can help reduce the temptation, demonstrating how the visibility of cues within our environment can dictate our actions.

Moving beyond physical spaces, the social environment also holds immense sway over our habits. The people we surround ourselves with can serve as powerful motivators or detractors in our journey toward habit formation. Research consistently illustrates that we tend to adopt behaviors and attitudes that align with those of our close social circles. If our friends prioritize fitness and healthy eating, we are more likely to engage in those habits ourselves. Conversely, if our environment is filled with negativity or unhealthy behaviors, those tendencies can seep into our own lives, making it challenging to maintain positive habits.

The concept of social accountability emerges from this understanding. Engaging in group activities or forming habit-oriented communities can create a support system that nurtures positive habits. When we commit to a fitness class with friends or join a book club, the collective commitment fosters a sense of accountability, making us more likely to adhere to our goals. This communal aspect of habit formation highlights the importance of aligning ourselves with people who reflect the behaviors we wish to adopt, showcasing the power of a supportive environment on our journey to self-improvement.

Another critical aspect of environment is its emotional resonance. Spaces have the ability to evoke feelings and memories, thus influencing our habits. For instance, a workspace suffused with personal items that remind us of our achievements can encourage productivity and creativity. On the other hand, environments that invoke stress or anxiety—such as a chaotic home life or a high-pressure job—can prompt coping mechanisms that may not align with our long-term goals. Therefore, recognizing how emotional responses to our environments shape our habits is essential for creating conducive surroundings that inspire and motivate.

Seasonal changes and their impact on our environment can also trigger shifts in habit formation. For many, the arrival of spring brings a sense of renewal and motivation, inspiring behaviors such as spring cleaning or outdoor exercises. Conversely, colder months might lead to a more sedentary lifestyle as people retreat indoors. Understanding these seasonal influences allows us to proactively adjust our environments to align with our goals throughout the year. Setting up a cozy reading nook for winter evenings or preparing an outdoor space for summer workouts ensures we are ready to embrace the habits we wish to foster, irrespective of the changing seasons.

Moreover, technology has transformed our environments in unprecedented ways, creating new dynamics in habit formation. The digital spaces we occupy—social media, apps, and online communities—have become integral to our daily lives. While technology can yield positive habit-forming tools, such as fitness trackers or productivity apps, it also presents challenges. The constant barrage of notifications and overwhelming content can lead to distractions, pulling us away from the habits we intend to cultivate. Thus, it becomes crucial to curate our digital environments as thoughtfully as our physical ones, allowing us to leverage technology in ways that support our goals rather than hinder them.

As we consider the multifaceted relationship between environment and habit formation, it's essential to recognize that we are not mere products of our surroundings, but rather active participants in shaping them. The act of consciously designing our environments demands intention and awareness. By identifying the habits we wish to cultivate, we can strategically modify our spaces—physical, social, and digital—to better align with those desires.

It is not merely about removing temptations or creating reminders; it's about crafting an ecosystem that nurtures the habits we aspire to develop. This intentionality involves regularly reassessing our environments, contemplating whether our spaces inspire us or constrain us. The journey towards effective habit formation is not static; it requires ongoing adjustments and adaptations as we grow and change.

Ultimately, understanding the power of our environment is a pivotal step in mastering habit formation. As we navigate through the complexities of daily life, we have the ability to harness our surroundings—both the tangible spaces we inhabit and the intangible networks we engage with—to construct an environment that fosters success. By remaining mindful of these influences, we can cultivate habits that are not only more attainable but also more sustainable in the long run. This understanding equips us to navigate challenges and embrace opportunities in our pursuit of growth and self-improvement, highlighting the profound impact our environments have on our everyday choices and, ultimately, our lives.

Creating a supportive environment for good habits involves making deliberate changes to both our physical spaces and our social contexts. These adjustments can significantly enhance our ability to establish and maintain positive behaviors. Here are several practical tips for optimizing your environment to foster good habits:

1. **Designate Specific Spaces**: Assign specific areas for particular activities.

For example, if you want to establish a reading habit, create a cozy reading nook in your home. This dedicated space serves as a visual cue that signals your brain to engage in reading whenever you enter that zone. Similarly, if you wish to exercise regularly, designate a specific area for workouts, whether it's a corner of your living room or a gym bag ready to go by the door.

2. **Minimize Distractions**: Identify elements in your environment that deter

you from your desired habits. For instance, if you find yourself distracted by your smartphone while trying to work, consider placing it in another room or using apps that limit your usage during work hours. Reducing these distractions can help you remain focused on the habits you are trying to develop.

3. **Use Visual Cues**: Take advantage of visual reminders to keep your goals

front and center. Post sticky notes with affirmations, reminders, or goals in places where you spend a lot of time, such as your bathroom mirror, refrigerator, or desk. These cues can reinforce your intentions and serve as prompts to engage in the desired habit.

4. **Organize Your Space**: A cluttered environment can lead to a cluttered mind, which in turn makes it harder to develop and maintain good habits. Spend some time decluttering your physical spaces. Keep only the items you need and that inspire you in view. When your environment is organized and visually appealing, you create a more conducive atmosphere for positive habits to thrive.

5. **Prepare Your Environment**: Set yourself up for success by preparing your environment ahead of time. If you want to eat healthier, stock your pantry and fridge with nutritious foods, and remove unhealthy options. Lay your workout clothes and sneakers out the night before so that they are readily available in the morning. The less effort it takes to engage in a good habit, the more likely you are to do it.

6. **Shape Social Circles**: Surround yourself with people who support and embody the habits you want to adopt. Research has shown that our habits are influenced by those around us. If your friends or family prioritize fitness, for instance, their behaviors can inspire you to exercise more. Engage in community activities or groups that align with your goals to foster a supportive social environment.

7. **Limit Negative Influences**: Just as you should seek out positive influences, it's equally important to minimize exposure to negative ones. If certain environments or groups of people encourage habits that you are trying to break, consider reducing your time spent there. This could mean avoiding fast-food restaurants if you are trying to eat healthier, or steering clear of social situations that revolve around excessive drinking if you are trying to cut back.

8. **Create Positive Rituals**: Establish routines that make use of your environment to reinforce good habits. For instance, if you want to cultivate a meditation practice, create a calming corner with cushions and candles designed solely for meditation. By creating a ritual associated with a specific location or items, you can make the practice feel special and inviting, making it easier to engage consistently.

9. **Utilize Technology Wisely**: In our digital world, technology can be both a distraction and a tool for habit formation. Use productivity apps and notifications strategically to remind you of your commitments and to help you track your progress. For example, habit-tracking apps can provide daily reminders and insights into your habits, reinforcing your commitment to maintaining them.

10. **Gradually Adapt Your Environment**: Start with small changes and observe their effects. Tackle one aspect of your environment at a time, making gradual alterations rather than overhauling your entire space at once. For instance, if you're aiming for a morning routine that includes meditation, start by altering your bedroom setup to welcome calmness and relaxation. Over time, as you see the positive effects of each small change, you'll feel motivated to implement more adjustments.

11. **Incorporate Nature**: Engaging with nature can have a significant calming effect and can stimulate positive habits. If possible, incorporate plants into your environment, whether at home or in your workspace. Studies have shown that greenery can improve mood, reduce stress, and promote well-being, all of which are beneficial for maintaining good habits.

12. **Review and Reflect**: Periodically assess your environment to see if it still supports your goals. As you grow and your habits evolve, your space may need to adapt. Take time to reflect on what is working and what isn't, and don't hesitate to make further adjustments as needed. Continuous refinement creates an environment that resonates with your journey toward positive habit cultivation.

By being mindful of your environment and actively shaping it to support your goals, you can create the perfect backdrop for nurturing the habits that will lead you to success.

The impact of social circles and peer influence on habits is profound and multifaceted. Our behaviors are often shaped not just by our own decisions, but also by the actions and attitudes of those around us. This is particularly evident in the nature of habits, which are often reinforced through social interactions and shared contexts. Understanding how social circles influence our habits can provide valuable insights into personal development and change.

The Role of Social Norms: Social norms dictate acceptable behavior within a group, and the influence they exert can significantly affect individual habits. When we observe those around us embracing certain behaviors, we are more likely to adopt similar practices. For example, if a peer group prioritizes healthy eating and regular exercise, individuals within that group are more inclined to follow suit. Conversely, if a social circle often engages in unhealthy behaviors, such as excessive drinking or smoking, those habits can readily become normalized and adopted. This illustrates that the environment created by our social circles can either foster positive or negative habits depending on the prevalent norms.

Peer Pressure: Peer pressure is often viewed negatively, but it is crucial to recognize its dual nature. While it can encourage unhealthy behaviors, it can also be a powerful motivator for cultivating good habits. Positive peer pressure occurs when individuals within a social circle encourage one another to engage in beneficial habits. For instance, friends who challenge each other to participate in fitness classes or join a book club can create an environment of accountability and motivation. This dynamic allows individuals to push beyond their comfort zones and achieve goals they might not have pursued alone.

Accountability and Support: Social circles can serve as important sources of accountability, providing encouragement and support as individuals work toward establishing new habits. When you make a commitment in front of others—say, by declaring your intention to run a marathon or to eat healthier—you're more likely to see that commitment through. The presence of supportive friends or family members can help maintain motivation, celebrate successes, and provide comfort during setbacks. This supportive network can serve to reinforce the behaviors necessary for maintaining habits over the long term.

Shared Experiences and Group Activities: Engaging in shared experiences or group activities can significantly bolster habit formation. When individuals participate in classes, clubs, or social initiatives that align with their desired habits, they create a sense of community that fosters motivation. The camaraderie formed in a running group, for instance, can inspire members to train regularly, while also creating friendships that strengthen adherence to healthy behaviors. Sharing in activities makes progress enjoyable and places less pressure on the individual to perform alone, creating a supportive atmosphere where everyone is working toward the same goals.

Encouraging Healthy Competition: Healthy competition can also arise within social circles, propelling individuals toward positive change. For example, friends might motivate one another by establishing fitness challenges, friendly contests, or goals that they aim to reach together. This competitive spirit can serve as a catalyst for action, making the process of habit formation engaging and dynamic. The energy generated by a little competition can infuse enthusiasm into the pursuit of good habits while fostering a spirited environment.

Observational Learning: Psychologist Albert Bandura's social learning theory emphasizes the importance of observational learning as a means of habit development. Within social circles, we unconsciously observe and imitate the behaviors of others; we learn from their successes and failures. If a friend posts their workout achievements on social media, it can inspire you to take similar actions. Seeing others transform their lives through healthy habits creates a sense of possibility, demonstrating that change is achievable and motivating you to embark on your own journey toward improvement.

Diversity in Influences: The composition of one's social circles can drastically influence habit formation. Engaging with diverse perspectives opens the door to new ideas and practices that one might not have previously considered. For instance, if you surround yourself with health-conscious individuals, the likelihood increases that you'll adopt their practices as well. Alternatively, a circle that lacks diversity may reinforce homogenous behaviors. Thus, consciously cultivating a variety of friendships across different interest areas can enrich your experience and help you incorporate new, beneficial habits into your life.

Emotional Support and Stress Relief: Managing stress is a key factor in maintaining healthy habits, and social circles play a crucial role in providing emotional support during challenging times. When faced with adversity, knowing you have friends who understand and empathize can make a world of difference. Supportive friends can act as a sounding board, providing advice, offering encouragement, and simply listening during tough times. This emotional safety net helps bolster resilience, making it easier to stay committed to your positive habits even when faced with life's ups and downs.

The Impact of Social Isolation: On the flip side, social isolation can have detrimental effects on habit formation. When individuals feel disconnected from others, it can lead to feelings of loneliness and despair, which may trigger negative behaviors such as unhealthy eating or substance abuse. A lack of social engagement can erode motivation and make it challenging to adhere to positive habits. Recognizing this dynamic emphasizes the importance of fostering connections and seeking out supportive relationships that combat feelings of isolation.

Choosing Your Circle Wisely: Ultimately, being mindful about the company you keep is essential for cultivating habits that serve your best interests. Surround yourself with individuals who inspire you, encourage growth, and celebrate your successes. It can be helpful to actively seek relationships with those who embody the qualities and habits you aspire to develop, as their influence will likely drive you toward your goals.

Navigating the intersection of social circles and habit formation highlights the intricate connection between our environment and behaviors. Understanding the power of peer influence not only empowers us to shape our habits more intentionally but also reminds us of the responsibility we hold within our social networks to foster positive change for ourselves and those around us.

Chapter 7: Habit Stacking and Automation

Habit stacking is a powerful strategy for establishing new behaviors by leveraging existing habits. The fundamental premise of habit stacking is simple: by attaching a new habit to a current one, we create a seamless transition that allows us to incorporate positive changes into our daily lives with minimal resistance. This method is particularly effective because it exploits the brain's tendency to follow established patterns, making it easier to initiate new behaviors without requiring excessive willpower or motivation.

The beauty of habit stacking lies in its accessibility; it does not demand the complete overhaul of our routines. Instead, it encourages us to look at our current habits from a new perspective, offering a structured approach that capitalizes on the automatic nature of our daily actions. For example, if you already have a well-established habit of brewing your morning coffee, you could stack a new habit, such as stretching for a few minutes, onto that routine. By consciously deciding to stretch immediately after you pour your coffee, you create a direct link between the two activities, effectively anchoring the new behavior to an already ingrained one.

To implement habit stacking, one of the first steps is to identify your current habits. Take stock of the behaviors you engage in consistently—these might be morning rituals, mid-day breaks, or evening routines. Once you have a clear understanding of your existing habits, the next phase is to choose a new habit that you wish to cultivate. Ideally, this new behavior should not require significant motivation or willpower; the more seamless the connection, the more likely it will stick.

The process of linking new habits to established ones can be enhanced through the use of an effective formula for creating a habit stack. A popular and effective way to frame this is to follow the structure: "After [current habit], I will [new habit]." This format not only provides a clear instruction but also reinforces the sequence of actions in your mind, making it easier to recall when it's time to enact the stack. For instance, you might say, "After I brush my teeth, I will meditate for five minutes." This clear directive encapsulates the cue (brushing teeth) and the desired action (meditating), creating a concise roadmap for behavior change.

It's essential to start small when creating your habit stack. Attempting to integrate too many new habits at once can quickly lead to overwhelm and frustration. By focusing on just one new habit at a time, you can ensure that you are able to manage and reinforce the connection between the existing habit and the new behavior. This approach also allows for better tracking of progress, as you can evaluate the effectiveness of each stack individually.

Moreover, the success of habit stacking can often be bolstered by committing to consistency. The psychological principle of consistency suggests that when we commit to a specific plan or behavior, we are more likely to follow through. By expressing a clear intention to perform the new habit immediately following the current one, we strengthen our resolve. The repetitive nature of this process will condition our brains to eventually recognize the two actions as part of a larger routine. Over time, the new habit will feel just as automatic as the one it is linked to, allowing it to effectively integrate into our lives.

Another significant aspect of habit stacking is the opportunity it provides for personalization. Not every habit stack will work universally; what matters are the habits that resonate with you and your daily rhythm. Personal preference should guide the selection of the new habit to ensure that it feels rewarding rather than burdensome. For example, if you love reading but struggle to make time for it, you might stack it with a habit you already perform regularly, such as having lunch. By telling yourself, "After I sit down for lunch, I will read for ten minutes," you're more likely to dedicate that time to your desired activity.

As you explore different combinations of current and new habits, you may find that experimenting with various stacks leads to unexpected and fulfilling outcomes. Some individuals discover that stacking habits in unconventional ways can yield incredible results, while others lean into more structured combinations. For instance, if they enjoy journaling but often forget to do it, they might connect it to their nighttime routine, saying, "After I wash my face, I will write in my journal." This connection effectively transforms a task that may feel burdensome into a pleasurable activity that emerges naturally from a consistent ritual.

Ultimately, habit stacking not only encourages the development of new routines but also reinforces the importance of flexibility and adaptability in our lives. Everyone's journey is unique, and the ability to modify and tailor habits according to personal preferences and lifestyle changes is vital in maintaining long-term success. As you embark on this process, regularly reassess your habit stacks for effectiveness and satisfaction. Are the new habits enriching your life? Are there adjustments you can make for better alignment with your needs and desires?

This reflective practice ensures that each stack works harmoniously, providing the opportunity for ongoing development and transformation without overwhelming you. By focusing on incremental adjustments and allowing yourself the grace to adapt, the philosophy of habit stacking becomes not merely a tool for self-improvement but a roadmap for personal evolution.

When it comes to automating positive behaviors through connected and stacked habits, the approach emphasizes the significance of linking new actions to existing routines in a way that creates a seamless flow in daily life. By harnessing the power of habit stacking, individuals can effectively design their lives to incorporate more positive actions without relying heavily on willpower or motivation. Here are several strategies to achieve this:

1. Create a Habit Chain

One powerful approach to habit stacking is creating a chain of linked behaviors, where one action naturally leads into the next. This strategy helps to create a fluid routine that feels cohesive. For example, suppose you are trying to establish a morning routine that includes drinking a glass of water, doing some stretching, and then writing in a journal. You could structure this as follows: as soon as you wake up (existing habit), you reach for a glass of water (new habit #1), then, after drinking water, you move immediately into a few minutes of stretching (new habit #2), and finally, you sit down to write in your journal (new habit #3). The success of this method lies in its simplicity—the transition from one habit to another becomes almost automatic, eliminating the need for conscious decision-making.

2. Align Actions with Daily Events

Another effective strategy is to align new habits with significant daily events or milestones that already occur in your life. By anchoring new behaviors to these moments, you create strong associations. For instance, if you want to incorporate gratitude into your daily routine, you could decide to reflect on three things you're grateful for every time you finish lunch. The act of finishing your meal serves as a cue to trigger this new habit. Similarly, if you aim to save money, consider transferring a set amount into savings every time you receive an alert for your paycheck or complete a purchase.

3. Use a Habit Tracker

Employing a habit tracker can significantly enhance the connection between stacked habits. By using an app, notebook, or calendar, you can visually track your progress as you establish new habits. For instance, if your stacked habits include taking a walk after lunch and reading for ten minutes afterward, you can mark off each completed action on a daily basis. The visual representation of your success can build momentum and motivation while highlighting the chain of habits you're cultivating. Over time, seeing your streak grow reinforces your commitment to these stacked behaviors, further automating the process.

4. Designate Specific Locations for Your Habits

Environmental cues are integral to habit automation. Designate specific locations for where specific habits will occur, creating associations that reinforce behavior. For example, if you want to start practicing a new language, set up a designated space in your home where you keep language-learning materials. Each time you sit in that space, you can engage in language practice after completing another existing habit, such as having your morning coffee. The location itself acts as an extra cue, nudging you to practice whenever you settle into that area.

5. Employ Time-based Stacks

Creating time-bound stacks is an effective way to structure behavior. By aligning habits with set times of day, you create a predictability that fosters routine. For instance, you may decide that after your morning shower, you will meditate immediately for five minutes, then review your goals for the day. The act of showering becomes the cue for both meditation and goal review. Over time, this structured stacking sets a rhythm to your day, making it easier to sustain those habits through the power of repetition.

6. Start Small and Gradually Build

To make habit stacking more manageable, start with small, attainable actions and build upon them gradually. If you're aiming to incorporate a new exercise regime, for example, begin with just two minutes of stretching each morning after you make your bed. As this stacks successfully onto your existing routine, you can gradually increase either the time or the intensity of the exercise. This incremental approach allows your brain to adjust and form connections between habits naturally, creating a sustainable routine.

7. Use Accountability Partners

Involving an accountability partner can streamline the automation of connected habits. When you share your goals with someone else, such as a friend or family member, you create an external cue for yourself. For example, if you and a friend commit to a habit stacking plan—like going for a walk after lunch together—you're more likely to stick to it due to the added layer of social commitment. The act of checking in with each other can further solidify the connection between your habits, making it easier to continue automating these behaviors through support and encouragement.

8. Reflect Regularly on Your Stack

In order to maintain effectiveness in habit stacking, taking time to reflect on your progress can reveal insights and new opportunities for optimization. Periodically check in to see how smoothly your habits are stacking together—are there any that feel awkward or clunky? Perhaps journaling about the effectiveness of your stacks could help identify which ones work best or need refining. Additionally, you may discover new opportunities to link additional habits together, facilitating a more profound automation of positive behaviors.

9. Celebrate Milestones

Recognizing and celebrating milestones is an important part of reinforcing stacked habits. When you successfully complete both the new and existing habits for a week, month, or longer, treat yourself to something rewarding, whether it's a day out, a favorite meal, or a small gift. Creating positive associations with completing your habit stack enhances the chance of repeated automated behavior by fostering a sense of satisfaction and fulfillment.

By utilizing these strategies to automate positive behaviors through connected and stacked habits, individuals can cultivate an environment that naturally encourages growth and improvement. This integrated approach to building routines not only increases the likelihood of success but also enriches everyday life by seamlessly incorporating positive habits into the fabric of daily activities. Through consistent practice and thoughtful stack design, anyone can develop a powerful toolkit for sustaining meaningful change.

To truly grasp the power of habit stacking, it's helpful to look at real-life examples where individuals have successfully linked new habits to existing ones. These stories illustrate not only the effectiveness of this technique but also its adaptability across various contexts.

One popular example is that of a health-conscious couple who wanted to increase their water intake. They chose to stack this new habit onto their existing morning routine. Each morning, after brushing their teeth, they set a glass of water next to their toothbrush. As soon as they finished brushing, they would drink the glass of water. This simple connection not only reminded them to hydrate but also turned it into a pleasurable morning ritual. Over time, the act of drinking water became automatic, seamlessly integrated into their start-of-day routine.

In the realm of fitness, many individuals find success through habit stacking with exercise. One notable instance is a busy professional who aspired to build a consistent workout routine but struggled to find time. She decided to link her new habit of exercising to her existing habit of watching television. Instead of plopping down on the couch at the end of a long workday, she committed to doing just five minutes of stretching or bodyweight exercises every time she turned on the TV. This small adjustment made her workout more engaging and less daunting. Before long, her body craved movement during those TV sessions, and she extended her routine beyond those initial five minutes, transforming sedentary TV time into an active, health-promoting habit.

Another example comes from a teacher aiming to foster a positive classroom environment. She recognized the importance of gratitude and wanted to instill this value not only in herself but in her students as well. To achieve this, she stacked the habit of expressing gratitude onto an existing daily practice: the morning announcements. Each day, before diving into the day's schedule, she introduced a "gratitude moment," where she and her students would share one thing they were thankful for. This practice created a ripple effect, encouraging students to reflect on positivity while simultaneously reinforcing her own commitment to gratitude.

The concept of habit stacking also extends into the digital realm. A tech-savvy entrepreneur wanted to be more mindful of his screen time and incorporate mental wellness into his daily routine. He decided to build a habit stack linked to his phone usage. When he unlocked his phone in the morning, the very first action he took was to engage with a meditation app for just two minutes. This small addition transformed how he started his day and reduced his urge to dive directly into work-related emails or social media, promoting mindfulness before engaging with the digital world.

In a household setting, parents often combine chores with enjoyable activities for their children. One father, seeking to teach his children responsibility, decided to stack the chore of washing the dishes after dinner with storytime. Every evening, he attached the new habit of storytelling to the existing task of cleaning up. While rinsing and drying the dishes, he would narrate a chapter from their favorite book. This not only made the chore more enjoyable but also fostered a love of reading in his children, successfully blending responsibility with bonding time.

Lastly, consider the case of an individual learning a new language. A college student determined to improve her foreign language skills chose to stack her language practice onto her morning coffee ritual. Each morning, while brewing her coffee, she would listen to a podcast in the target language. This seamless integration made language learning a part of her daily routine, and soon, she found herself eagerly anticipating her morning ritual, transforming her commute into a productive learning experience.

These examples demonstrate that habit stacking can lead to transformative changes in daily routines, helping individuals cultivate positive behaviors without added stress. Whether it's related to health, personal development, or relationship building, linking new habits to existing ones offers a practical framework that fits seamlessly into our lives. By observing how others have successfully implemented these changes, we gain valuable inspiration to craft our own personalized habit stacks, paving the way for meaningful progress in our pursuits.

** Chapter 8: Case Studies of Transformation **

In this chapter, we will explore the inspiring stories of individuals who have successfully changed their habits, each carving a unique path toward personal growth and transformation. These narratives highlight not only the struggles faced during the process but also the profound triumphs that emerge when commitment and resilience converge. Each case underscores the idea that while the journey may be fraught with challenges, the rewards of cultivating new habits are immeasurable.

Case Study 1: Sarah's Journey to Health

Sarah, a 34-year-old marketing professional, found herself trapped in a cycle of unhealthy eating habits and sedentary behavior. Working long hours at her desk led to frequent takeout meals and minimal physical activity. Over time, she noticed her energy levels plummeting, and with it, her self-esteem. With a family history of health issues, she knew she needed to make a change.

The turning point came during a routine health check-up when her doctor warned her about her rising cholesterol levels and potential weight gain. Determined to alter her trajectory, Sarah began her journey by identifying small, manageable habits to implement. She started with the "two-minute rule," opting to walk for just two minutes every day during her lunch break. As those two minutes transformed into five, then 10, and ultimately 30, Sarah's confidence bloomed. Eventually, she phased out takeout meals, choosing to meal prep on Sundays, which empowered her to make healthier choices throughout the week.

Sarah's story illustrates the power of incremental change. By setting realistic goals and gradually increasing the complexity of her routines, she not only lost weight but also gained a newfound appreciation for her body and its capabilities. Her case reminds us that the path to transformation often starts with small, consistent steps.

Case Study 2: Robert's Financial Awakening

At 40, Robert found himself drowning in debt, overwhelmed by credit card bills and back-to-back financial mistakes. His typical response to stress involved shopping sprees and impulsive buying, creating a cycle of temporary satisfaction followed by crippling regret. After a particularly harsh conversation with his partner about their finances, Robert recognized he needed a significant shift in his approach to money management.

Determined to reclaim control, Robert began by tracking his spending habits for a month, meticulously logging every expense. This exercise revealed surprising patterns, including discretionary spending that had ballooned his debt. The key components of Robert's transformation stemmed from setting strict financial goals and creating a budget that allowed for both essential and discretionary spending, thus crafting a framework within which he could thrive.

To solidify his new habits, Robert enacted a "30-day spending freeze," where he committed to refraining from non-essential purchases. This period of reflection helped him understand the emotional triggers behind his spending habits. Over time, he gradually integrated a practice of mindful spending, focusing on intentional purchases that aligned with his values. Through a commitment to learning about financial literacy and enlisting the help of a financial advisor, Robert successfully climbed out of debt and began investing in his future. His story emphasizes that financial health is closely tied to cultivating mindful habits and understanding one's motivations.

Case Study 3: Maria's Quest for Balance

Maria, a 28-year-old teacher, struggled with work-life balance. Her dedication to her students often led her to bring work home, sacrificing her personal time and well-being. Overwhelmed and burnt out, Maria realized that her passion for teaching was beginning to fade under the weight of perpetual stress and exhaustion.

In her quest for equilibrium, Maria initiated a rigorous self-reflection process to identify the habits that contributed to her burnout. She recognized that her inability to say no and her habit of overcommitting were major culprits. Seeking to combat this cycle, Maria adopted several new practices. She began by establishing clear boundaries regarding work hours and committing to a daily "unplug" hour—an hour spent away from work distractions and dedicated to her own well-being.

She further incorporated mindfulness practices such as meditation and yoga into her daily routine. The insightful practice of journaling also became a catalyst for her transformation, allowing her to articulate her thoughts and feelings, which relieved some of the stress she had carried. With time, her boundaries and self-care routines flourished, restoring her enthusiasm for teaching and creating space for personal activities that reignited her joy. Maria's journey demonstrates the importance of self-awareness and proactive measures in establishing a more balanced and fulfilling life.

Case Study 4: Jake's Professional Reinvention

Jake, a 45-year-old software engineer, found himself stagnating in his career. Despite his technical skills, he struggled with public speaking and networking, which limited his opportunities for advancement. Frustrated but determined, he resolved to confront these habits head-on.

Jake started by enrolling in a local public speaking course, committing to practice in a supportive environment. Each week, he was pushed out of his comfort zone, which helped him build confidence in articulating his ideas. Additionally, Jake began attending industry meetups, initially feeling out of place but gradually finding common ground with fellow professionals. Utilizing the habit loop framework, Jake identified his cues—feelings of anxiety before events—and replaced them with new routines, such as deep breathing exercises and positive affirmations.

Over time, his efforts began to pay off. Not only did he develop a stronger public speaking presence, but he also expanded his professional network and gained skills that positioned him for a promotion. Jake's transformation serves as a powerful reminder that facing fears and discomfort head-on can yield extraordinary outcomes.

Case Study 5: Emma's Emotional Resilience

Emma, a 30-year-old writer, battled anxiety and negative self-talk that stifled her creativity. In a profession where rejection is commonplace, her inner critic often overshadowed her achievements and potential. Looking to reclaim her narrative, Emma sought support from a therapist and began a rigorous personal development journey.

Central to her transformation was the habit of practicing gratitude. Each morning, she started a gratitude journal, jotting down three things she appreciated about herself and her life at that moment. This practice helped shift her focus from self-doubt to recognizing her worth and accomplishments. Furthermore, Emma adopted a routine of morning affirmations, which fortified her resilience against negativity.

As her mental habits evolved, Emma found herself pursuing new creative endeavors without fear of failure, launching a blog that resonated with many readers seeking empowerment through vulnerability. Her journey underscores the profound impact of emotional habits on one's personal and professional life, demonstrating that changing the inner dialogue can lead to transformative outcomes.

Case Study 6: David's Social Awakening

David, a 38-year-old introvert, often felt isolated and disconnected from friends and family. His habit of avoiding social engagements stemmed from a profound discomfort in navigating social interactions, which he attributed to his introverted nature. After a particularly lonely holiday season, he decided to confront this aspect of his life.

David began by setting small, attainable social goals, such as reaching out to one friend each week. He used technology to his advantage, scheduling video calls that felt less daunting than in-person meetings. Additionally, he joined a local book club where he could engage with others around shared interests, thereby easing the pressure of one-on-one interactions.

As David's social circle began to expand, he became more comfortable expressing himself in various settings, ultimately leading to stronger connections. This growth transformed his weekends from solitary ones to engaging social experiences. His story serves as a testament to the idea that stepping out of one's comfort zone can yield profound personal connections and enrich life experiences.

These stories illustrate the diverse ways individuals have taken control of their habits to foster transformation and growth. Each case offers valuable insights into the struggles people often face while highlighting the determination required to create lasting change. With commitment and a clear understanding of the mechanics behind habit formation and modification, anyone can embark on their own transformative journey.

In examining the stories of individuals who have successfully changed their habits, it becomes evident that the journey towards transformation is filled with both struggles and triumphs. Each case highlights the intricacies of human behavior, the resilience required to tackle deeply ingrained habits, and the profound sense of accomplishment that comes from overcoming obstacles. Lets take a closer look at the past case studies:

Case Study 1: Sarah's Journey to Health

Sarah's transformation was not merely a physical journey but a battle against deeply ingrained habits and the psychological barriers they imposed. Each day spent at her desk felt like a direct confrontation with her past choices—culinary convenience marked by greasy takeout and an unshakeable lethargy that shadowed her once-active lifestyle. The struggle to maintain motivation was real, exacerbated by the long hours and fatigue that accompanied them. Sarah had moments of doubt, where she would catch herself yearning for the instant gratification of takeout rather than the effort of cooking. It was during these moments that she grappled with her self-worth; each unhealthy choice felt like a small defeat in her broader quest for health.

However, as she began implementing small changes, those incremental victories became pivotal. The initial two-minute walk was not just a physical exercise; it became a metaphor for her journey. At first, the two minutes felt like a daunting task, a reminder of how far she had fallen from her former self. Yet, as she pushed through those initial struggles, she found joy in the simple act of moving her body outside of the confines of her office. The triumphs she experienced—progressively increasing her walking time—fortified her resolve, igniting a simmering motivation that slowly replaced her previous feelings of inadequacy.

The challenge of meal prep was similarly daunting. The first few Sundays felt like an exhausting chore. Sarah had to navigate a new approach to planning and organizing her week, diving into recipes and grocery lists while battling old cravings for takeout. There were days when the effort felt overwhelming, particularly when faced with the convenience of ordering food rather than cooking. However, as she began to see the fruits of her labor—both in her improved health and her reflection in the mirror—her commitment deepened. The shift from reliance on unhealthy choices to embracing nutritious, home-cooked meals marked a significant psychological breakthrough for Sarah. Each meal she prepared became a point of pride, a testament to her perseverance against the tide of her previous habits.

Case Study 2: Robert's Financial Awakening

Robert's journey towards financial freedom was fraught with emotional turmoil and confronting uncomfortable truths. Initially, the act of tracking his spending brought up feelings of shame; each entry in his spreadsheet was a stark reminder of the accumulation of his past mistakes and impulsive choices. This exercise was not merely a logistical task, but an emotional reckoning with his financial irresponsibility. The numbers did not lie, revealing a cascade of blind spending that created a chasm of debt.

Within this struggle, Robert faced the challenge of redefining how he viewed money. It was a vehicle for satisfaction, but also an anchor pulling him under. The fight against the instinctual urge to shop during moments of stress was monumental. Each shopping spree provided a fleeting thrill, but ultimately deepened his sense of despair. The "30-day spending freeze" served as a crucible of sorts, where Robert had to grapple with his impulses head-on, giving him the space to reflect on his emotional triggers without the crutch of immediate gratification. Initially, the freeze felt suffocating; he frequently experienced urges to spend, battling both temptation and the creeping anxiety that came from confronting, rather than avoiding, his issues.

Progress came with moments of insight. The emotional relief of acknowledging the root causes behind his spending patterns opened up new pathways for behavior change. Each mindful purchasing decision made after the freeze was a small victory, reinforcing a burgeoning sense of financial empowerment. The shift from impulse to intention wasn't instantaneous, but each day offered an opportunity for reflection and growth.

Case Study 3: Maria's Quest for Balance

Maria's pursuit of work-life balance was punctuated by the ebb and flow of her dedication to her students against the candid reality of her own well-being. The struggles she faced were not only external—stemming from workplace expectations—but also deeply internal. The act of bringing work home became a suffocating norm. Maria had to confront the guilt that surfaced whenever she thought of prioritizing her own needs over her responsibilities to her students. Each time she chose to work late or took on an extra project, it felt like a betrayal to her personal life; the imbalance festered as her passion waned in the face of exhaustion.

Identifying boundaries became a pivotal point in her transformation process, leading to an ongoing internal dialogue about worthiness and the need for self-care. Establishing her "unplug" hour was less about the hour itself and more about the significant implications it carried—an acceptance that she deserved time for herself. Initially, when she switched off her work devices, anxiety washed over her; how could she take a break when there was still so much to do? The struggle to disengage from work-related thoughts often intruded on her unplugged moments.

Yet, as she committed to this segment of self-care, Maria discovered pockets of tranquility that revitalized her spirit. Embracing practices like meditation took effort; the initial silence felt foreign and uncomfortable, filled with racing thoughts that seemed to fight against her attempts at calm. Over time, those moments transformed into periods of reflection and clarity, helping her understand what truly mattered beyond her professional obligations.

Incorporating yoga into her routine was another struggle. Each session was a confrontation with both physical limitations and the mental noise she carried.

Maria learned to view each yoga practice as an opportunity to release tension rather than an obligatory task. Gradually, her emotional resilience blossomed, tethering her journey towards a balanced life with renewed enthusiasm for teaching.

Case Study 4: Jake's Professional Reinvention

Jake's professional stagnation cast a long shadow on his self-esteem. Each day spent at his job felt like a reminder of his limitations—public speaking anxiety gripped him tightly, framing the opportunities he yearned for as insurmountable challenges. The dread of networking events loomed large, as he often spiraled into feelings of inadequacy, leading to avoidance. The effort it took to break free from these limiting beliefs felt overwhelming, as his inner critic constantly questioned his readiness to face such emotional hurdles.

Despite the daunting realities, Jake's decision to enroll in public speaking courses marked a defining moment of proactive choice, but it was far from a panacea. The initial sessions were fraught with discomfort and self-doubt. Each new lesson nudged him further out of his comfort zone, filling him with apprehension but also a flicker of hope. The pivotal moments were punctuated by stumbles, moments in which words escaped him or nerves overtook his performance; yet, each setback served as a stepping stone towards greater resilience.

Jake faced his anxiety by embracing his discomfort and focusing on the incremental changes he could make each week. The process of attending networking events became a challenging yet crucial practice. Initially, he felt out of place and awkward among seasoned professionals, but these experiences highlighted the necessity of stepping into social settings to dismantle the fear that had held him captive.

Utilizing the habit loop framework was transformative for Jake. By identifying triggers, he began to circumvent cycles of anxiety with actionable strategies, reinforcing a sense of control over his narrative—a powerful turnaround from helplessness to agency. Each practice moment, whether in public speaking classes or industry meetups, built his confidence incrementally, culminating in increasingly seamless interactions. With time, he transformed not only his presence in meetings but also his perspective on career advancement, reshaping the way he perceived social engagement.

Each case exemplifies the intricate tapestry of struggles and triumphs woven together in the fabric of personal transformation. The journey is rarely linear, marked instead by a series of ups and downs that each individual must navigate in their pursuit of meaningful change.

The journeys of Sarah, Robert, Maria, Jake, Emma, and David provide valuable insights into the transformative power of habits. Each case not only highlights unique challenges and contexts but also reveals essential lessons that can be applied universally.

1. The Power of Incremental Change

Sarah's journey emphasizes that significant transformation often begins with small, manageable changes. Her experience illustrates that setting realistic goals and gradually increasing the complexity of routines can yield astonishing results. This incremental approach reduces the psychological barriers to change, making it more approachable and sustainable. Individuals can take inspiration from Sarah's strategy of starting small—whether it's committing to a brief, daily walk or meal prepping once a week—and build from there to achieve greater health and confidence over time.

2. Mindful Awareness and Tracking

Robert's story underscores the critical role of self-awareness and accountability when changing financial habits. By meticulously tracking his spending for a month, he identified patterns that he had previously overlooked. This practice of awareness is universally applicable across various aspects of life. Whether we are aiming to improve health, productivity, or relationships, keeping a record of our behaviors can unveil insights that guide us toward positive changes. The importance of reflection should not be underestimated; it helps illuminate our habits' roots, triggers, and consequences.

3. Boundaries and Balance

Maria's experience highlights the necessity of setting boundaries to foster a more balanced life. Her dedication to her students came at the expense of her own well-being, leading to burnout. This balance is an essential lesson for many professionals who may sacrifice their personal lives for their careers. By committing to a daily "unplug" hour and practicing self-care, Maria showed that boundaries are not just protective measures but essential components of a fulfilling life. Her story teaches that taking time for oneself not only enhances personal well-being but also allows individuals to show up more fully in their commitments.

4. Facing Fears and Discomfort

Jake's path to professional reinvention illustrates the necessity of confronting one's fears head-on. Many individuals face similar discomforts in their careers, whether related to communication, leadership, or networking. Jake's choice to enroll in public speaking courses and attend industry meetups signifies a proactive approach to personal growth. His success reinforces the idea that discomfort often precedes growth, and confronting that discomfort can lead to enriching experiences and development. The lesson here is clear: stepping out of one's comfort zone can unlock doors to opportunities that once felt unreachable.

5. The Impact of Emotional Habits

Emma's quest for emotional resilience reveals the profound influence of our inner dialogue on our lives. Her practice of gratitude and morning affirmations catalyzed a shift from self-doubt to self-acceptance. This relationship between emotional habits and overall well-being is crucial, particularly in creative fields or high-stress environments where self-criticism can be prevalent. Her journey teaches that cultivating positive emotional habits is not just about resisting negativity; it's about actively fostering a sense of positivity and appreciation, which can lead to greater creativity and fulfillment in life and work.

6. Building Connections through Vulnerability

David's social awakening highlights the importance of vulnerability in forging connections. Often, individuals refrain from reaching out due to preconceived notions about social interactions or their introverted nature. David's method of setting small, achievable social goals allowed him to ease into more fulfilling relationships. His journey teaches us that establishing genuine connections often requires deliberate effort and a willingness to engage with others, even when it feels uncomfortable. Vulnerability can deepen relationships, foster empathy, and create a strong sense of community, enriching our lives significantly.

Each of these case studies reveals that change is a multifaceted and often non-linear process. The individuals mentioned navigated their unique challenges with determination, self-reflection, and a willingness to adapt. They learned that true transformation comes from understanding the underlying mechanisms of their habits, fostering self-awareness, and cultivating positive, supportive environments.

By highlighting the importance of small, consistent changes; the value of mindfulness in tracking behaviors; the necessity of boundaries for balance; the courage to face one's fears; the power of emotional habits in shaping our narrative; and the significance of vulnerability in building connections, these journeys provide a robust framework for anyone seeking to make meaningful changes in their lives. They remind us that irrespective of the domain—health, finances, work, emotions, or relationships—habits are at the core, and changing them can set the stage for profound personal and professional growth.

Chapter 9: Maintaining and Evolving Habits

The significance of adapting and evolving our habits over time cannot be understated. As we journey through life, our circumstances, priorities, and aspirations shift. What initially served us well may no longer align with our current needs or goals. Habits are not static; they are dynamic elements of our behavior that require thoughtful reflection and periodic adjustment. By embracing the idea that our habits should evolve, we allow ourselves the flexibility necessary to thrive in an ever-changing world.

Our environments continuously change in ways that impact the habits we form and maintain. Perhaps a new job presents different challenges and demands that require a realignment of our daily routines. Or maybe significant life events—such as moving to a new city, starting a family, or nearing retirement—compel us to rethink the structures we've established. Habits that once felt beneficial can morph into obstacles without due consideration. Therefore, a regular reassessment of our habits is essential for ensuring they remain relevant and effective.

This evaluation process is rooted in self-awareness. As we develop greater awareness of ourselves, we may find that certain routines have become obsolete, or worse, detrimental. Take, for example, a once-empowering morning workout routine that has begun to feel burdensome. If that routine no longer energizes us or contributes positively to our mental and physical health, it's time to adapt. Perhaps it's time to exchange high-intensity workouts for gentler exercises like yoga or walking, or it could be beneficial to shift the workout to a different time of day when energy levels are higher. By being attentive to how our habits serve us, we can ensure they continue to align with our evolving self.

Moreover, the nature of our goals is ever-changing. A person who once aimed to improve their physical health may find that their priorities shift to fostering deeper relationships or furthering their career. In these situations, maintaining the same habits without adaptation can lead to stagnation and discontent. One must examine the habits that originally contributed to the achievement of past goals and critically consider whether they are still conducive to new endeavors. If our goals evolve but our habits remain rigid, we risk falling short of our potential and succumbing to frustration.

The interplay between habits and identity is also crucial to understand. As we grow, we often redefine who we are and who we aspire to be. If our habits are not congruent with this evolving identity, a dissonance can arise. For instance, someone who has embraced the identity of a lifelong learner may find that binge-watching television contradicts their new self-image. This conflict can trigger feelings of guilt or inadequacy, which can further hinder our ability to change. Thus, maintaining habits that resonate with our current self-concept is fundamental for emotional and psychological well-being.

In addition to considering external circumstances and personal identity, the demands of life can change in ways that necessitate habit evolution. For instance, new responsibilities, such as caring for children or aging parents, or shifts in work-life balance, may require individuals to revamp their routines. What once fit seamlessly into our daily lives may now require reevaluation. Engaging in reflection allows for strategic adjustments that honor our new realities while still driving progress toward our goals.

Strategies for harnessing the flexibility of habits include implementing regular check-ins with ourselves. Setting aside time—be it weekly, monthly, or quarterly—to assess the effectiveness of our habits can provide crucial insights. During these reflections, we can ask ourselves probing questions: Are these habits still serving their intended purpose? How do they contribute to my overall well-being and fulfill my long-term aspirations? What changes can I make to align them more closely with my current goals? By creating a habit of self-reflection, we can progressively adapt our routines to better match our evolving lives.

Another key factor in the importance of habit evolution is the concept of experimentation. Embracing a mindset of trial and error can empower us to explore new habits or tweak existing ones. There may be a sense of fear surrounding change; after all, we often clench tightly to familiar routines. However, viewing habit adjustment as an experimental process—a series of hypotheses to be tested—removes the pressure surrounding perfection. By treating habit evolution as a natural progression, we open ourselves to a wealth of opportunities for growth and development.

Integrating feedback from trusted sources such as friends, family, or mentors can also elucidate the need for habit evolution. These external perspectives can offer valuable insights and highlight areas we may have overlooked. A candid conversation with a close friend about how your current work-life balance affects your well-being may unearth revelations that prompt you to rethink your commitments and routines.

Moreover, fostering a growth mindset related to habits encourages resilience, reinforcing that setbacks are not failures, but rather bridges to understanding what adjustments are necessary. Viewing challenges as part of the process helps create a more compassionate approach toward ourselves and our habits. In this mindset, experimentation and adaptation cease to be daunting; instead, they become opportunities for personal exploration.

As we navigate the fluid landscape of our lives, the importance of maintaining habits that adapt and evolve over time emerges clearly. By recognizing that our habits are not merely tools for achieving static goals, but rather living aspects of our journey, we can engage with them more thoughtfully. By committing to continuous reflection, remaining open to experimentation, and embracing the changes required for growth, we set the stage for habits that not only persist but flourish alongside us.

Strategies for Long-Term Commitment, Including Reflection and Adjustment

Creating new habits is an important step, but maintaining them over time is where the real challenge lies. The initial excitement of a new routine can quickly fade, and without strategic approaches to reinforce commitment, even the best intentions can fall by the wayside. To sustain habits, individuals need a framework that encourages ongoing reflection and adaptation, ensuring that habits remain relevant and beneficial throughout life.

Establishing Regular Check-Ins

One of the most effective strategies for long-term commitment is to establish regular check-ins with oneself. These sessions could take the form of weekly or monthly reviews, allowing time to reflect on progress, assess the impact of habits, and make necessary adjustments. During these check-ins, individuals can consider questions such as:

- What habits have I been successful in maintaining, and how do they positively impact my life?
- Are there habits that no longer serve my goals or feel relevant? If so, how can I modify or replace them?
- What challenges have I encountered in maintaining my habits, and how can I address them?

Setting aside dedicated time for these reflections can cultivate a deeper understanding of one's habits and foster a proactive mindset toward personal growth.

Emphasizing Flexibility

Rigid adherence to a specific routine can lead to frustration or burnout, especially when life circumstances change. Adapting habits in response to shifting priorities or new environments is essential for long-term success. Flexibility allows individuals to reassess what they want to accomplish and adjust their habits accordingly without feeling like they have failed.

For instance, if a person has committed to a daily workout but finds that their schedule no longer allows for a full hour at the gym, they might adapt by incorporating shorter, more efficient workouts—such as quick bodyweight exercises at home. This flexibility can keep motivation high and prevent discouragement from setting in.

Incorporating Feedback Mechanisms

Feedback is a powerful tool for maintaining habits over time. By incorporating mechanisms that deliver regular insights into progress, individuals can keep their goals in sight. This could involve keeping a journal where daily or weekly accomplishments are recorded, utilizing habit-tracking apps that provide data on consistency, or even seeking accountability from friends or mentors.

The act of reviewing feedback can also serve as a motivational booster, providing tangible evidence of progress and areas for improvement. When people can see how their efforts are contributing to their goals, it reinforces their commitment to the habits they have chosen.

Celebrating Milestones

Celebration is often overlooked, yet it is crucial for maintaining motivation over the long haul. Recognizing milestones—whether big or small—can infuse the habit process with positivity and encourage continued effort. Make it a point to celebrate when certain thresholds are reached, such as sticking with a new morning routine for 30 days or completing a month of daily meditation.

Celebration doesn't have to be extravagant; it can be as simple as treating oneself to a favorite snack, taking a moment to savor the progress made, or sharing achievements with a supportive peer group. These celebrations keep the journey enjoyable and engender a sense of accomplishment that reinforces the habit.

Leveraging Environmental Cues

Since habits are often linked to specific environmental cues, deliberately shaping one's surroundings can help sustain long-term behavior changes. This might mean designating a particular space in the home as a reading nook to promote a reading habit or leaving running shoes by the door as a reminder to exercise.

Making the desired behavior more accessible and reducing barriers can increase the likelihood of following through. Conversely, it may also involve removing cues that prompt negative habits—such as not keeping junk food at home or avoiding places that trigger unhealthy behaviors—allowing individuals to focus on their positive routines.

Building a Support System

Having a robust support system can dramatically influence the sustainability of habits. Engaging with groups, whether in-person or online, provides opportunities for shared experiences, advice, and encouragement. These connections create a sense of accountability and community, aspects often lacking when individuals must rely solely on themselves.

Mentorship, whether formal or informal, can contribute to long-term success as mentors can provide insights based on their experiences and offer guidance during challenging times. Plus, celebrating each other's successes creates a culture of positivity that further reinforces commitment to personal growth.

Practicing Self-Compassion

Along the journey of maintaining habits, sometimes things don't go as planned. Life can become hectic, and slip-ups are inevitable. Practicing self-compassion during these moments is essential. Instead of falling into a cycle of self-criticism, individuals can view setbacks as natural breaks in the road rather than a definitive end to progress.

A self-compassionate approach encourages individuals to recognize their humanity, allowing for mistakes without completely derailing their commitment. A quick shift in perspective can turn a moment of failure into a learning opportunity. What can be learned from the misstep? How can it inform future actions? Treating oneself with kindness during difficult times fosters resilience and a greater likelihood of re-engaging with habits after encountering obstacles.

Adapting Goals and Challenges

Just as personal circumstances evolve, so too should the habits and goals that accompany them. Setting long-term goals is essential, but it's equally important to break them down into smaller, actionable steps that reflect changing priorities and interests. Regularly revisiting and updating these goals keeps them fresh and meaningful.

Including new challenges or variations in routines can also be beneficial. For instance, if someone has been consistently exercising but feels bored, introducing new activities—such as joining a dance class, hiking, or trying out a new sport—can reignite enthusiasm and commitment to physical activity.

Embracing Lifelong Learning

Finally, nurturing a mindset centered on lifelong learning allows for the continuous evolution of habits. This involves staying curious about oneself, exploring new strategies, and being open to trying new approaches. Attending workshops, reading books on personal development, or participating in training programs can offer fresh perspectives that not only improve existing habits but also inspire the creation of new ones.

By consciously committing to reflect, adjust, and evolve, individuals can maintain their habits over time, ensuring that they serve their changing needs, aspirations, and contexts. This ongoing journey of self-discovery fuels personal growth, allowing habits to adapt alongside personal development.

A growth mindset, a term popularized by psychologist Carol Dweck, refers to the belief that abilities and intelligence can be developed through dedication, effort, and perseverance. When applied to habits, this mindset encourages individuals to view challenges and setbacks as opportunities for learning and improvement rather than as roadblocks to success. Cultivating a growth mindset related to habits is essential for maintaining motivation, fostering resilience, and enabling continuous evolution in one's life practices.

To foster a growth mindset regarding habits, one must first recognize that habits are not static entities. They are dynamic and can adapt in response to changes in our lives, environments, and goals. This understanding shifts the perception of habits from mere routines to evolving systems that can be optimized for better performance and personal satisfaction. For instance, a person may establish a running habit but later realize that the initial routine no longer serves their health needs or aligns with their current lifestyle. Embracing a growth mindset encourages them to reassess their approach, perhaps experimenting with varying distances, changing locations, or incorporating different forms of exercise.

An important part of fostering a growth mindset is the practice of self-compassion. Instead of berating ourselves for lapses or regressions in habit formation, it's vital to approach these moments with a sense of kindness and understanding. Self-compassion allows us to recognize that everyone faces challenges in their journey of habit formation and that setbacks are an integral part of growth. This perspective can alleviate feelings of guilt or shame and motivate us to recommit to our goals with renewed vigor.

Furthermore, embracing a growth mindset requires an openness to feedback and self-reflection. Regularly assessing our habits can help us identify patterns, successes, and areas for improvement. Reflective practices, such as journaling or meditative contemplation, invite moments of clarity where we can evaluate what is working and what is not. This explicit reflection allows us to make informed adjustments and highlight the progress made, reinforcing the notion that growth is a continuous journey rather than a destination.

Encouraging experimentation is another crucial aspect of fostering a growth mindset around habits. The willingness to try new approaches or modify existing ones can lead to breakthroughs in habit evolution. For example, if an individual has established a healthy eating habit that has become monotonous, introducing new recipes, cuisines, or meal-prepping techniques can reignite enthusiasm and motivation. Experimentation not only fosters creativity but also helps break the monotony that can lead to disengagement from our routines.

In addition to personal experimentation, drawing inspiration from others can greatly enhance the growth mindset related to habits. Engaging with communities or networks that share similar goals can provide fresh perspectives, strategies, and support. When individuals exchange experiences, they often discover new methods of habit formation that resonate with them, further fueling their commitment to growth. This sense of belonging and shared purpose can be a powerful motivator, creating a collective drive to evolve habits for personal betterment.

Crucially, acknowledging the role of effort in habit formation is a cornerstone of the growth mindset. Understanding that mastery takes time and that perfection is not the goal can alleviate pressure. When facing obstacles, reminding ourselves that effort, persistence, and the willingness to adapt are what ultimately lead to success allows us to stay engaged in the process. Celebrating small wins along the journey reinforces the belief that progress is possible and motivates continued effort.

Moreover, reframing challenges as opportunities is an essential strategy in cultivating a growth mindset related to habits. Instead of viewing difficulties as signs of failure, recognizing them as valuable lessons can reshape how we approach our routines. Each challenge presents a chance to learn something new about ourselves and our habits. For example, if a setback occurs, such as slipping back into an old habit, it can serve as a prompt to investigate the underlying reasons. Are there external triggers? Emotional responses? This active inquiry into our habits fosters a nurturing environment for growth, allowing us to redefine our approaches in ways that are constructive and enriching.

In promoting a growth mindset, individuals should also aim to set process-oriented goals rather than solely outcome-oriented ones. While outcome goals can serve as motivating markers, focusing on the process—the small, actionable steps that lead to those goals—encourages a healthy mindset around habit formation. For instance, rather than solely aiming to lose a set number of pounds, an individual might commit to cooking a nutritious meal three times a week or walking a certain number of steps daily. This shift places emphasis on the journey and the routines created, which can be more sustainable and rewarding over time.

Ultimately, cultivating a growth mindset around habits intertwines with self-awareness, compassion, and curiosity. Recognizing that each person's journey is unique promotes a sense of individuality that celebrates personal rhythm and pace. It empowers individuals to embrace their paths and to know that evolution is an integral part of the human experience. Allowing for flexibility within habits opens the door to continuous improvement and adaptation, encouraging a lifelong commitment to growth and well-being.

In this context, the relationships we form with our habits can also influence our mindset. When we approach habits with a sense of curiosity, viewing each habit as an experiment in personal growth rather than a rigid rule, we enhance our ability to evolve. This playful attitude towards habits invites exploration and reinforces the idea that we can always choose to start anew.

Embracing a growth mindset creates a framework that transforms the approach to habit formation into a holistic, resilient practice. Instead of merely striving for immediate results, this perspective fosters an understanding that effective habit change is an ongoing process filled with opportunities for learning and development. It encourages individuals not just to maintain their habits but to actively engage in the art of discovering, redefining, and evolving themselves through their daily practices. It is this journey of adaptation that ultimately leads to profound change and richer, more fulfilling lives.

Conclusion

As we reach the end of this exploration into the profound influence of habits on our lives, it becomes evident that understanding and harnessing the power of habits is not just an academic exercise; it is a transformative journey that can redefine personal and professional growth. Throughout this book, we have navigated the intricate landscape of habit formation, delving into the science behind how habits are formed, the neurological processes at play, and the impact they have on our daily lives.

We began with **Chapter 1**, where we uncovered the fascinating workings of the brain—specifically, the roles played by the basal ganglia and the prefrontal cortex in shaping our routines. This foundation set the stage for our understanding of how habits are ingrained in our neural pathways and why they can be so challenging to alter. Through various studies and research findings, we gleaned insights into the brain's response to repeated behaviors, laying the groundwork for the practical applications that followed.

In **Chapter 2**, we introduced the concept of the habit loop—a framework that illustrates the components of cue, routine, and reward. By dissecting each part of this loop, we gained clarity on how to identify triggers that initiate our habits, analyze the behaviors that result, and understand the rewards that reinforce our actions. The inclusion of real-world examples enriched this discussion, showing how individuals in various contexts successfully navigated their own habit loops.

With a firm grasp of the mechanics of habits established, **Chapter 3** empowered readers to take stock of their own behaviors. We provided actionable tools for tracking and assessing personal habits through techniques such as journaling and the use of habit tracking apps. The enriching case studies showcased in this chapter illustrated that transformation is indeed attainable and offered a pathway for readers to begin their own journeys of self-discovery.

In **Chapter 4**, we focused on the proactive process of building new habits. The strategies discussed emphasized the significance of small changes, particularly the "two-minute rule," which encourages starting new behaviors on a manageable scale. We highlighted the importance of consistency and patience, underscoring that meaningful change is often a gradual process built on repeated efforts.

Conversely, **Chapter 5** tackled the critical process of breaking bad habits. We explored techniques to recognize negative patterns and eliminate them from our lives while emphasizing the integral role of accountability and social support in this endeavor. Furthermore, we provided practical alternatives for replacing detrimental habits with healthier choices, reaffirming that achieving positive change often involves proactive substitution rather than mere elimination.

In **Chapter 6**, we examined the influence of our environments on habit formation. The insights offered various strategies for creating supportive surroundings that foster good habits. By altering our physical spaces and being selective about our social circles, we can significantly enhance our capacity for positive change.

Building on this foundation, **Chapter 7** introduced the innovative concept of habit stacking—linking new habits to existing ones to facilitate effortless integration into our routines. This chapter provided strategies for automating positive behaviors and shared inspiring real-life examples of effective habit stacks, demonstrating that this method can lead to substantial behavioral shifts without overwhelming effort.

Chapter 8 brought forth compelling case studies of transformation, showcasing individuals who successfully changed their habits and their lives. Their stories revealed the struggles and triumphs inherent in the habit-changing process, offering valuable lessons on resilience, commitment, and the possibility of transformation through deliberate action.

Lastly, in **Chapter 9**, we discussed the importance of maintaining and evolving habits over time. Embracing a growth mindset allows us to continuously reflect on our practices, making necessary adjustments in response to life's changing circumstances. Long-term commitment, active reflection, and a willingness to adapt were emphasized as crucial elements of sustaining positive habits well into the future.

The journey to mastering habits is both an art and a science; it requires understanding the neurological and environmental underpinnings as well as personal dedication and adaptability. We encourage you to take actionable steps toward your own habit journey. Whether you aim to cultivate new positive habits, break free from destructive ones, or sustain and evolve the changes you've made, the resources provided within this book can guide your efforts.

As you move forward, remember that transformation is possible. You hold the power to reshape your daily actions, influence your future, and enhance your overall quality of life through intentional habits. For further reading and support on this journey, I recommend exploring additional resources that delve deeper into habit science, personal development, and behavioral change.

Thank you for embarking on this habit formation journey, and may your newfound knowledge inspire lasting change and growth in your life. The power to redefine your habits—and, in turn, your future—is in your hands!

Appendix

Suggested Reading List on Habits, Productivity, and Psychology

1. **"The Power of Habit: Why We Do What We Do in Life and Business" by Charles Duhigg**
- Duhigg explores the science behind habit formation and how understanding the habit loop can lead to meaningful change.

2. **"Atomic Habits: An Easy & Proven Way to Build Good Habits & Break Bad Ones" by James Clear**

- Clear provides actionable strategies for habit formation, emphasizing the power of small changes and the significance of identity in building lasting habits.

3. **"Mindset: The New Psychology of Success" by Carol S. Dweck**

- Dweck introduces the concept of growth vs. fixed mindsets and how our beliefs about our abilities can influence our potential for change.

4. **"Better Than Before: Mastering the Habits of Our Everyday Lives" by Gretchen Rubin**
- Rubin offers insights into the different tendencies people have when it comes to habits and provides a roadmap for making and breaking them based on personal tendencies.

5. **"The 7 Habits of Highly Effective People: Powerful Lessons in Personal Change" by Stephen R. Covey**
- Covey's classic book outlines foundational habits that foster personal and professional effectiveness.

6. **"The 5 AM Club: Own Your Morning. Elevate Your Life." by Robin Sharma**
- Sharma shares the transformative power of morning routines, advocating for early rising as a means to improve productivity and overall well-being.

7. **"Tiny Habits: The Small Changes That Change Everything" by BJ Fogg**

- Fogg presents the Tiny Habits method, focusing on how small changes can lead to significant behavioral shifts.

Worksheets for Habit Tracking and Reflection

- **Habit Tracker Template**: A printable template to help you track your daily habits. It includes sections for setting goals, monitoring progress, and reflecting on successes and challenges.

- **Weekly Reflection Worksheet**: This worksheet encourages you to evaluate your habits at the end of each week. It prompts you to assess what worked, what didn't, and how to adapt your strategies moving forward.

- **Goal Setting Worksheet**: A guided format to help you outline your intentions related to habit development, including specific goals, actionable steps, and timelines.

- **Cue and Reward Journal**: A dedicated space to record the cues and rewards associated with your habits. This worksheet will help you identify patterns in your behavior and make necessary adjustments.

Online Resources and Communities for Support

- **Tiny Habits® Community**: An online platform where you can join like-minded individuals who are focusing on making small, sustainable changes in their lives.

- **The Habit Coach Podcast**: Hosted by Ashdin Doctor, this podcast offers tips, insights, and strategies for building and maintaining good habits.

- **Reddit - r/habits**: A supportive online community where users share their experiences, challenges, and successes in building and breaking habits.

- **Facebook Groups**: Search for groups dedicated to habit formation and personal development where members share tips and encourage each other throughout their journeys.

- **Habitica**: An app that gamifies habit tracking, allowing you to create a personalized avatar and gain rewards for completing tasks and forming new habits.